IN CONSTANT PRAYER

Also by ROBERT BENSON

Between the Dreaming and the Coming True

Living Prayer

Venite: A Book of Daily Prayer

The Night of the Child

The Game: One Man, Nine Innings, a Love Affair with Baseball

That We May Perfectly Love Thee

The Body Broken

A Good Life

Home By Another Way

Daily Prayer

Digging In

IN CONSTANT PRAYER

robert benson

THOMAS NELSON
Since 1798

NASHVILLE DALLAS MEXICO CITY RIO DE JANEIRO BEIJING

Published in Nashville, Tennessee, by Thomas Nelson. Thomas Nelson is a registered trademark of Thomas Nelson, Inc.

Thomas Nelson, Inc., titles may be purchased in bulk for educational, business, fund-raising, or sales promotional use. For information, please e-mail SpecialMarkets@ThomasNelson.com.

All Scripture quotations are the author's paraphrase.

All prayers from the liturgy of the hours have been adapted from *The Book of Common Prayer of the Episcopal Church of America.*

The sample daily office in appendix A is taken from Robert Benson, *Daily Prayer.* Raleigh, NC: Carolina Broadcasting & Publishing, 2006. www.dailyprayerlife.com. Used by permission.

Page Design by Casey Hooper

Library of Congress Cataloging-in-Publication Data

Benson, R. (Robert), 1952-
      In constant prayer / Robert Benson.
          p. cm.
      ISBN 978-0-8499-0113-3 (hardcover)
      ISBN 978-0-8499-2108-7 (IE)
      1. Prayer—Christianity. 2. Divine office.
I. Title.
BV215.B423 2008
248.3'2—dc22
2008003176

Printed in the United States of America
08 09 10 11 RRD 5 4 3 2 1

*This book is for my friends at the
Cathedral Parish at Ninth and Broadway.*

*And it is for The Friends of Silence and of the Poor,
whoever and wherever you may be.*

By tradition, going back to early Christian times, the divine office is devised so that the whole course of the day and night is made holy. . . . It is the very prayer which Christ Himself, together with His body, addresses to the Father.

—THE ENCYCLOPEDIA OF THE CATHOLIC CHURCH

CONTENTS

FOREWORD

ALMOST FOUR DECADES AGO, THE LATE ROBERT WEBBER gave contemporary Christians two of the greatest summarizing phrases of our faith in those early postmodern, post-Christendom times. He said more and more of us were becoming "evangelicals on the Canterbury trail" and that what we were pursuing was—and is—intimate contact with the "ancient future."

Webber was right. He was right both descriptively and prophetically. More and more of us have been indeed returning in thought and in practice to the ancient disciplines of the faith, to ways of being that would accompany, compliment, and complete our ways of believing.

The first of the ancient practices to command our attention was fixed-hour prayer . . . or the keeping of the offices . . . or the observing of the divine hours. . . . There are many names for it, but they all refer to the same thing. They all refer to the practice of interrupting secular time every three hours for the observance of worship time made sacred by prayer.

During the mid- to late 1990s, a veritable plethora of prayer manuals was published in the United States and abroad for use, both lay and clergy, both private and corporate, in observing the hours. Robert Benson, long an observer of the hours, compiled one of those manuals, as did I and a number of others who likewise were lifelong practitioners of the discipline.

As interest grew and matured, theologian Scot McKnight gave the twenty-first century another gift by writing *Praying with the Church*, in which he distinguished between praying *in* church and praying *with* the Church. In clear and impassioned detail, McKnight developed the theology and the effectual difference between the two forms of worship.

Now, some five or six years later, Robert Benson returns to the conversation bearing yet another gift. With *In Constant Prayer*, he brings to us the poetry of fixed-hour prayer. In his skilled, vulnerable, gentle hands, the divine hours become not only divinely beautiful, but also totally accessible to every desiring, hungering Christian. What he accomplishes here is no less than the laying bare in beauty of the ancient practice which itself most grants the soul the experience of beauty.

For such as teacher as this, all the Church should be grateful.

Phyllis Tickle
General Editor
Ancient Practices Series

1

ONE TRUE THING

Tell them what you have seen and heard.
—Jesus of Nazareth

We believe that the divine presence is everywhere. . . .
But beyond the least doubt we should believe this
to be especially true when we celebrate the divine office.
—The Rule of Saint Benedict

I think it would be well, and proper, and obedient, and pure,
to grasp your one necessity and not let it go, to dangle
from it limp wherever it takes you. Then even death,
where you are going no matter how you live, cannot you part.
—Annie Dillard

I have a friend named Bettie who lives in Alabama. I pray for Bettie by name a lot of days, not because I think that she needs my prayers, but because I want to be sure God remembers that I am a friend of Bettie's.

A priest told me once that he did not think God had favorites. But, he told me, with a twinkle in his eye, he is pretty sure God has special friends. If that is true, then Bettie may well be one of them.

If I could pray like Bettie, I would not likely be writing this book about these things.

This is a book about the most ancient practice of Christian prayer, a way of prayer known as the *daily office*. It is known by other names as well—the *liturgy of the hours*, *fixed-hour prayer*, the *divine office*, the *canonical hours*, the *divine hours*, *daily prayer*. Its roots are firmly planted in the early Church, and it has become, in recent years, the focus of a great deal of interest among people who grew up in Christian traditions in which such a way of prayer was not a part of their ongoing prayer life.

That was certainly true for me. I stumbled into the daily office when I was almost forty years old. And I have never quite recovered.

I spent two years as part of a community of sixty-five people known as the Academy for Spiritual Formation. Our Academy met for a week each quarter. We spent our days learning about the history and traditions of Christian prayer and how to transpose some of that wisdom and practice into the busy and noisy lives of us modern folks.

I finished the Academy some fifteen years ago now. The world of prayer and contemplation to which the Academy introduced me still draws me deeply, and I am still fooling with all of this, still convinced that there are deep truths buried here if I can just be smart enough or patient enough or devout enough to dig them out.

I am not much holier than I was before I began, but I am still trying nonetheless.

During those weeks in the Academy, each day would begin before breakfast with morning prayer at seven. We would say vespers together and take Holy Communion together as the sun was going down and dinner was being prepared. The day would end with night prayer at nine thirty—the offering of confessions and praise—completing our day's journey and taking us into the Great Silence, where we slept and waited for the whispering of the Voice over the dark and the void, waited for God to say, "Let there be light" again.

I wish I were poet enough to take you back there with me.

We said our prayers together in this great room, large enough to hold four hundred people if the chairs were in rows the way they set them for camp meetings. The room was paneled in old pine with great beams above us. It was the way all old campground chapels should be. The place has been there since the '30s, I think. As my father might say, there was laughter in those walls—and there were tears and prayers and praises and hymns and shouts and sorrows in there too. I used to sit in there at the altar for hours some nights.

For the Academy, the chairs were arranged in a circle of two rows, with an opening at one end for the procession of the candle or the gifts for the Table. At the other end was the Table itself. No matter where you sat, you were always looking into the faces of your fellow pilgrims. No small comfort, that.

I cannot fully express what it meant to me to say the office twenty times in a week with those brothers and sisters. If I sit still enough just now, though, I can still hear them singing the psalms and saying the Gloria, making their way through the liturgy together with care and joy. I can hear the silences, even.

Bettie was a part of the same community. At the end of each day, we would meet in small groups to process the day's information and to encourage one another in the new bits and pieces of our spiritual journey. Then we would share prayer requests and pray around the circle.

Bettie would say something like, "Jesus, help Alan's back to feel better in the morning," and in the morning Alan's back would feel better.

Or she'd say, "Jesus, help Robert not to worry," and the next day I would not be so anxious.

One day, after six days of torrential rain, she said, "Jesus, we need good weather tomorrow for traveling home," and the rain stopped before any of us had time to say amen. I swear it did, and I have witnesses.

Over the years, whenever something untoward or difficult would happen to one of us in the group, someone would call Bettie to tell her so she could pray for us. Invariably, she always knew about it before anyone called her. It was among the most powerful things I have ever seen. It was also a little scary sometimes.

There are those among us for whom the life of prayer, a life of close communion with God, a life in which there is a simple faith and a simple conversation that goes on with the One who made us, takes place in an extraordinary way. There is no doubt about that. There are one or two folks like that in your church as well. They are not always the ones who are asked to pray in public, but they are the ones you call when something terrible has happened.

If you are one of those people, I may well have very little, if anything, to teach you about prayer. Except to say, of course, that my back is sore and I am worried about some of the stuff I am saying here and I have not seen the weather forecast but I could use a few sunny days if it is not too much trouble.

If you are one of those people, you know it. And you know that most of what I have to say about prayer may have meaning only for the rest of us.

I grew up in a church crowd where the Bettie way of talking with God was expected of all of us all of the time. Even those of us who were not like Bettie at all.

So I would pray like Bettie, and nobody's back ever got better, and the rain did not stop. The problems never got solved, the fears never went away, and the healing I prayed for so fervently never came. I began to believe that prayer would not make any difference, or it would not make any difference if I was the one doing the praying. For a while I believed that I just needed to pray louder or shed more tears. Later I began to believe that it was because God would not listen.

I have finally come to believe that it was because I was trying to say Bettie's prayers, not the ones I could say.

When I first stumbled onto this way of participating in the life of prayer, this way of prayer I had unknowingly been searching for until I finally stood still long enough for it to find me, I thought I had found something that was just for contemplative folks like me. I was pretty certain it was for us poets and shy people, people who preferred silence to conversation and chose stillness over action.

So I went charging back into my local parish to try to change everyone into contemplatives like me. All I needed to do was to get them to quit their jobs and stop being extroverts and a raft of other things I thought were necessary to becoming, as Dostoevsky said, a monk hidden in the world who waters the earth with his tears.

I did not get very far. The extrovert thing is as strong as the introvert thing, I came to discover. I knew it was louder; I just did not realize the degree to which I was outnumbered. It turns out I am on the tip of a very tiny iceberg. According to the psychologists, only one person out of every hundred is as introverted as I am.

So I backed off for a bit, self-righteously thinking that such prayer was just for us chosen few (there is a confession in there, if you listen carefully), just for the enlightened, we who would rise up, all seven of us, and pray the Church into sanctity in our time.

I am coming to believe that this way of prayer may not be for the Betties of the world, those who are numbered among God's special friends, the ones with whom God seems to converse in an astonishing way. Except for those times when, like Bettie, their journey crosses paths with ours, and they are given to us as gifts to be beside us for a time.

I also have come to believe that this ancient way of prayer is not just for the contemplatives of the world, either, the particular and peculiar few who are called to live in monastic communities or to wear habits or collars or some such thing. It is not just for those of us who do not make small talk because we cannot make small talk, who would rather be alone than in a crowd, and who are even more alone when we are in a crowd. We are drawn to such prayer more easily, perhaps, but it is not just for us.

The prayer of the office is not for everyone. But that is not to say that it is only for a minority of us. The prayer of the office is not just for God's chosen few, and it is not only for God's special friends. It is prayer for the rest of us.

It always has been. For thousands of years, the daily office has been a primary way to hold ourselves in closer communion with the One who made us. It is a way to sanctify our days and our hours, our work and our love, our very life itself.

It is for any of the rest of us who need to find a way to pray. It is for those of us, and this includes most of us, who cannot pray Bettie's prayers and yet must find a way to respond to our calling to pray without ceasing.

In the simplest of terms, the daily office is a regular pattern and order for formal worship and prayer that is offered to God at specific times throughout the course of the day. Each set of prayers, known as an *office*, is made up of psalms, scriptures, and prayers. It is the sort of prayer that is most often associated with monastic communities and the more liturgical and sacramental parts of the Church.

What I hope to do here—with as little jargon and technical talk as possible—is to open up some of the mystery of the daily office for those who have had little or no exposure to this ancient way of Christian prayer.

I hope to shed some light on the history of the daily office and about the call to prayer it offers to us in our time. I will say some things about the obstacles that keep us from participating in such prayer and some of the ways we might overcome them. I will also share something about the benefits that can accrue to us as pilgrims, as members of the community of faith, and as the whole body of Christ if we begin to participate in this ancient tradition that has sustained the Church through the ages.

In a way, I hope to write the book I could not find when I first stumbled into the daily office all those years ago.

Some of you who read this work will be somewhat familiar with what is written here. For others, some of the information and ideas will be very new and, in some cases, very startling. Some will have already begun to pray the office and are looking to learn more about this way of prayer you have come to hold dear. Some will have only just begun to learn of its existence and are in search of hints and clues as to how to keep exploring in the right direction. Still others will find all of this completely new and more than a little bewildering.

However you come to these pages, I recommend a posture that includes one part openness, one part faith, and one part welcome. There is a possibility that some new thing is about to unfold before you even though you may not yet perceive it, as the prophet Isaiah once said about a deeper mystery. This way of prayer—the prayer that has sustained the life of the faithful for centuries—has a way of sneaking up on you and not letting go. Which is what often happens when we come in contact with God. Communion with God is several things—predictable is not one of them.

You should know that I do not consider myself a scholar. I think of myself as a poet and a storyteller. I do not stand in the pulpit; I sit in the pew. I am not a seminarian or a cleric or a professional religious person of any sort. I began my journey in the direction of a deeper prayer life as a pilgrim with some questions and a fountain pen and a lot of time on my hands, armed with little more than a desire to see what might happen to me if I learned to pray the prayer that has been prayed by the community of saints for centuries.

I would not even now consider myself to be a person of prayer. I am not even certain that I can fully describe what all of these things have come to mean to me.

What I know of prayer has come from reading books and asking questions, from talking with those who have come from church traditions other than mine, and from wandering and wondering with other pilgrims for whom this way of prayer has become a central part of their life with God. And from participating in the prayer itself.

I have stories to tell that I believe give voice to or shine some bit of light on the questions that surround this way of prayer, questions that usually seem to arise in the hearts and minds of those who are drawn to it. I know such questions lived in me when I began this journey. They were forming in my head and in my heart and in my very soul from the moment of my first exposure to this way of prayer. And maybe some of them are your questions as well.

"To be a writer," said the novelist Ellen Douglas, "is to bear witness to all that you have seen and heard." A writer is all I really make any claim to be. And so I am bound to tell these stories to you and even again to myself.

Perhaps in the reading, and in the telling, new words and notions and questions about prayer will rise up in us both. I certainly hope so.

I have written about some of these things before, in bits and pieces in other books. There is a sense in which I have been writing this book for more than fifteen years. Not long enough to know everything about this great mystery, and not long enough to become much more than I was when I started—a pilgrim who wants to learn how to live a life that is shaped by and around and for prayer, a life that becomes a prayer that is prayed without ceasing. I have to tell you that the whole business still astonishes and terrifies me; it still lifts me up and manages somehow to pull me forward, or if not forward, then maybe even higher or closer or nearer to the One who made us and to whom we pray.

I have been at it long enough to know at least this: of all the things I have ever written about or will ever write about, this is the one true thing that has come to matter to me the most.

2

ANCIENT PRAYER FOR THE ANCIENT OF DAYS

Stand at the crossroads and look; ask for the ancient paths, ask where the good way is, and walk in it, and you will find your souls.
—The Prophet Jeremiah

These then are the tools of the spiritual craft. When we have used them without ceasing, day and night . . . our wages will be what the Lord has promised.
—The Rule of Saint Benedict

Say the words of the ancient prayer, and listen for the prayer of God that rises in your heart.
—Fr. Edward J. Farrell

My wife and I are newspaper people; we keep up with three or four of them. Even when we travel, our newspaper habit has become so ingrained in us that one of my first moves in the morning is to head out the door in search of the papers. If I find the *New York Times*, I get bonus points.

When we are home, a day has not really begun properly until I have traveled a few blocks through our neighborhood to a corner market to pick up the day's papers. We are not the only household with morning rituals. Some folks turn on the radio or the television or simply open their front doors to retrieve their newspapers from the porch.

I have to drive to get our newspapers because the *Times* has not yet decided to confer deliverable-area status on the sixteen square blocks that we call home. I could move four blocks in any direction, and they would be happy to drop off my *Times* at my front door. But as it is now, we are undeliverable. I had a preacher say that about me once when I was younger—un-deliverable.

One of my friends suggested that I walk to the store to get the papers so I would get some exercise and feel better. I told him to mind his own business. If I walked to get the papers, given all the papers I get, I would end up not only walking but weight lifting too, and the whole business sounds dangerously healthy to me. So I drive.

One block north, two blocks west, and another block north gets me down Twelfth Avenue. Every morning, as I turn left off of Twelfth, I see a crowd of folks getting into their cars. There are usually a couple of dozen or so. They are in the parking lot of a house of worship, and they have been to morning prayers. And I not only see them climbing into their cars between 6:30 and 7:00 on Sabbath days, but on Tuesdays and Wednesdays and every other day of the week as well.

Sometimes I go west a few blocks before I go north, and when I do, I dead-end into Belmont Boulevard. Across the street, there is a small crowd of folks piling into their cars as well. They have been to church for prayers already that morning, and they will be there again tomorrow morning when I come by, and the day after that too.

A few more blocks west, I pass yet another parking lot, with yet another crowd of people who have been up early in the morning to say prayers together before the day begins.

Sometimes I think I might like to leave a little earlier for the papers and join with some of those folks for prayers. But I will not ever do that, I expect. There are some good reasons.

The first crowd I pass is leaving the mosque in my neighborhood. We wave at each other as I drive by, but I do not have the uniform or the theology to go in.

The second crowd is a Catholic one, and though I would

be welcome there, it would not be quite the same. Eventually, there would be a moment when they would invite people to come to the Table, and I would be left out.

The third group meets at the synagogue, and I'm not Jewish.

When I see those three groups in the morning at those places, I do not know if there are hundreds more like them at dozens of places that I do not drive past in the morning, or if I am driving past the whole praying universe. I do not know if they are the tip of the iceberg or the whole iceberg.

But I have a suspicion that if there is a crowd at those usual gathering spots that early in the morning, then there is also an unseen crowd gathered somewhere—in different rooms together, shall we say—who are saying the prayers as well.

Now, as to the houses of worship I drive by whose parking lots are empty in the morning, I do not want to speculate, of course.

Sometimes, when I see those three crowds of folks in the mornings, it makes me think things that both trouble me and make me wonder. I have some things in common with them. I, too, am awake and on the streets before the sun is up. And I like to go to sacred rooms, too, and join my voice with the saints whenever they are marching in or out or wherever it is we are all headed.

Another thing I have in common with them is this long historical connection back through the centuries to the people of Abraham and to the practices of prayer of the faithful and the sometimes not-so-faithful. It is a connection that goes back at least six thousand years.

When we ask where the daily office came from, "the people of Yahweh" is the first answer. "The Psalms" is the second answer—Psalm 119, to be exact. That is where the notion of daily fixed-hour liturgical prayer began. "Seven times a day," wrote the psalmist, "will I rise to praise your name." Our Jewish mothers and fathers in the faith, the first people to worship the God we worship, took the notion seriously. The first written versions of daily fixed-hour worship and prayer date back to some four thousand years before Christ.

Taking their cue from the psalmist, the Hebrew people developed a set of daily liturgical offices of prayer. These little prayer services were to be said at specific times of the day, or specific "hours," if you will: daybreak, before the workday began, noon, midafternoon, sundown, before bed, and midnight.

The liturgies for those prayer services opened with a call to prayer. Introductory psalms were said or sung as an invitation into the presence of God. A hymn of praise and formal prayers were said for particular seasons and holy days and the time of day itself. The office included a regular cycle of readings from the Holy Scriptures. Each office was said in much the same way worship services are structured in the more formal traditions of the modern Church.

These hours of prayer observed in places of worship and in homes, in large crowds and small, at the appointed hours of the day—day after day, week after week, month after month, year after year—were the ongoing daily offering of praise and worship offered to God by the people of God. It shaped them as a culture and as a religious community.

The bells would ring and the shops would close, candles would be lit, and whatever else was part of the office for that time of day would be done. The Hebrew people would set aside whatever was at hand and pray the liturgy for the hour. In larger cities and towns, some of the day's prayers would be offered at synagogues; in Jerusalem, they would be offered at the temple. The settings varied from village to village and home to home.

This offering of ongoing praise and worship to the One who made us gave shape and structure to the ordinary life of the day itself. There were Sabbath days and feast days and other holy days when other liturgies were said and sung. But the people's ongoing life together was shaped by the daily prayer. It sustained them as a community of faith.

The practice of this continuous life of worship was so central to the Hebrews' individual and collective life with God that four thousand years later, they were still teaching it and performing it and learning it and perfecting it when the Messiah actually came among them. Not many people recognized him then; they just thought he was a carpenter's son from Nazareth, so they taught him the prayers. He, too, would have joined with those who said the prayers of the faithful. That is likely what was going on in the synagogues and in the temple when he went there to pray, as the Scriptures tell us he did. It is where the young Jesus would have heard the Scriptures and prayed the psalms and learned the ways of the devout.

For the most part, the first Christians were Jews. The coming of the Messiah was not the end of the story of the God they had known; it was a new chapter in that same story. So even as they wrestled to find language and ritual to reflect this new and astonishing way of God being with them, the early Christians continued to do what Yahweh's people had always done—they rose seven times a day to praise the name of the Lord. No one said that now they had Jesus, there was no need to worship God.

I expect the words of the liturgies began to change some, since the Messiah had now come, but the followers of Christ did not stop praying the prayers that offered ongoing, daily praise and worship to the One who promised and then sent the Messiah to them. If one would not offer worship and praise to God now, after what God had just done, then exactly when would one offer such a sacrifice of praise?

Daily hours of prayer, in fact, were chief among the things that held Christian communities together during the early years of the Church and the years of persecution. The stories of Paul and Peter and the rest in the early days of Christianity, the stories in the book of Acts, often mention this disciple or that one going to the temple to pray at a specific hour. They were not casually dropping by for a visit; the bells had rung, and the hour of prayer was at hand. The daily prayers were said, often in secret once the persecutions were begun, as an act of praise and devotion, and as a way of strengthening and sustaining one another in the daily struggle to remain faithful in the face of great odds.

After a few hundred years of folks being killed because of their Christian faith, the Roman emperor Constantine declared Christianity the state religion of the empire. The gospel spread even more quickly to the Gentiles, people for whom such a life of prayer was not part of the fabric of their society. And there was no longer a need for these prayers to be said in secret; they could be said in the churches springing up all over the empire. Gradually, and perhaps imperceptibly, there was less need to say the prayers for the strength to hold Christians to one another, and so the practice began to fade.

The fourth and fifth centuries mark the appearance of the *abbas* and the *ammas,* men and women who moved to the desert to live in monastic communities where the ancient traditions could be held dear and the daily office could be said. The offering of daily praise and worship to Yahweh had begun to move from being a practice for all the faithful to becoming a practice for just a few.

If it were not for the monks and nuns, the practice of daily prayer might well have died out altogether. For hundreds of years, in monastic settings large and small, the ancient practice of daily prayer was shaped and reshaped, the liturgies written and rewritten, the rituals and customs adapted and readapted. During the Middle Ages, as the influence of monastic communities grew, and as monks and nuns became part of local church communities, the prayers were offered in churches where they were available to laypeople once more. Shorter versions of the offices began to appear, versions for laypeople as well as clergy.

Hold on tight—we're headed into the Reformation, during which all manner of things that had to with the ancient Church were set aside for various reasons. Some of those reasons were theological, some were political, and the rest were somewhere in between. "Beyond here be dragons," goes the saying. This is not a book about all of that, and I recommend we leave those discussions to the professionals who seem to enjoy arguing over such things. What matters here, in this story, is what happens to the practice of praying the hours.

It is worth noting that if you look at the prayer books of many Protestant groups in the early post-Reformation world—

the Lutherans and the Anglicans and the Methodists, for example—the liturgies for daily prayer are in all of those prayer books.

In the post-Reformation world of Europe, some parts of the Church ended up with a professional class whose responsibility it was to offer the daily prayer. Part of that class were the monks and nuns; the other part was the clergy. And provision was made for laypeople to participate as well.

But once the Church crossed the pond and entered the New World, the whole notion of the responsibility for offering the daily prayers, at least as far as the American Protestant world was concerned, got left behind somehow. These things were still in the prayer books but not on the radar. Since the fourteenth century, we Protestants by and large do not even expect professional clergy to say the prayers anymore.

In a very different context, the singer Michelle Shocked once said, "Politics and art are too important to be left to the professionals." This is not a jab at professionals; it is a call to amateurs.

The daily prayer of God's people—the divine office, the liturgy of the hours, the work of God, morning and evening prayer, whatever name you want to use for it—is too important to be left to the professionals anyway.

The truth is that the divine office was never meant to be just for professionals, or to be prayed just by a few. It was meant to be prayed by all the faithful, or at least it has been for six thousand years. It was meant to be part and parcel of our individual piety and our common life of devotion. It was meant to be offered by all of us.

For some five hundred years, the vast majority of Protestants have not offered up the prayer that those who came before us did, the prayer that sustained and shaped the early Church, the prayer that kept the Church alive during the centuries, "the very prayer which Christ Himself, together with His body, addresses to the Father."

We who claim to follow Yahweh, we who long to follow in the steps of the faithful who went before us, we who so often talk about learning to more fully live the life shown to us in the stories of the early Church, we do not participate in this part of the tradition of worship and prayer they passed down to us.

And now some of us are being drawn to this ancient way of offering praise and prayer and worship to the Ancient of Days.

3

THE DAILY OF THE DIVINE OFFICE

Accept the willing tribute of our lips and teach us your ways.
—THE PSALTER

*Those who have been sent on a journey are not to omit
the prescribed hours but to observe them as best they
can, not neglecting their measure of service.*
—THE RULE OF SAINT BENEDICT

*Antoine likened monks to oarsmen on a ship, lifting a sheet
to catch a sacred wind, the breath of something holy.*
—REMY ROUGEAU

THE TRADITION OF SAYING THE DAILY OFFICE HAS LAN-
guished for so long that many of us have barely heard of it, if
at all, and not many of us know what these hours of prayer in-
volve. Even if we have heard of the daily office or had some
exposure to it, there is a long list of questions that come to
mind for many of us at the beginning of our journey in the
direction of such prayer.

What follows falls somewhere between a primer and a
crash course. It is a rough sketch of the daily office as it is most
commonly practiced today.

First things first. I should remind you of the origins of the
ancient prayer itself: "Seven times a day will I rise to praise
your name." The faithful followers of Yahweh took it seriously
and literally. But with the exception of certain monastic communities, we Christians seem to have gotten over the "seven
times a day" part a long time ago.

The hours are indeed still observed seven times a day in
many monastic settings, settings where the community exists pri-
marily to say the prayers. In such places, a monk or a nun's day
still includes *Lauds, Prime, Terce, None, Sext, Vespers,* and *Compline,*
the traditional names for the hours.

For practical reasons—life outside a monastery being very much different from life inside one—the specific prayers and other content of the daily office were condensed and reshaped through the years into a set of four offices—morning, noon, evening, and night prayer. The condensing and reshaping of the offices is clear in the breviaries and prayer books from the years immediately following the Reformation.

For Christians in our time, laity and clergy alike, who seek to participate in the daily prayer of the Church, there is plenty of freedom to choose a regimen that allows for the shape and pace and structure of our individual daily lives. Most commonly, the call is to practice the discipline of morning and evening prayer. We are the ones who are living the day; it is up to us choose the specific times of the day when we will say the prayers that sanctify the day unto the One who gave it to us.

Now we will look at what makes up a single office, a single hour of prayer. (A sample divine office can be found in appendix A, if you would like to follow along.)

The term *hour of prayer* derives from the notion of a bell ringing the hour of the day at a particular time and in a particular way as a call to prayer. To "pray the hours" does not mean that it takes sixty minutes to properly say a single office. Indeed, it takes considerably less time, depending on the version of the office one uses.

The word *office* is rooted in the Latin word *opus*; the same root gives us the word *offering*. The word *liturgy* means "the work of the people," and if part of the work of faithful people is not to offer ongoing daily praise and worship to the One who made us, then I do not know what else we are supposed to be up to here. The marriage of those two ideas—office and liturgy—seems appropriate to me.

Each office in the cycle of daily prayer is rooted in the same basic pattern, in the same sort of way that most Sunday worship services are built on the same pattern, regardless of the community in which we worship. To be sure, there is some variation from one version of an office to the next, in the same way Sunday morning worship varies within the Church. Communities will have differences as to which parts of the office come first or second, but there is a kind of general shape to an office that has been handed down to us over the centuries. In any of the prayer books we use, we can be confident that we are praying in essentially the same sort of way as have God's people for centuries on end.

An office begins with a *versicle* or call to prayer, such as, "Open our lips, and our mouths shall proclaim your praise." Sometimes these sentences are different according to the season of the church year or the specific office or day. You will see the versicles called by different names as well—the "preparation" or "request for presence," for example.

The versicle is followed by the *venite*, or psalm of invitation.

Certain psalms are associated with certain times of the day and therefore with particular offices. "Come let us raise a joyful song, a shout of triumph to the rock of our salvation"—the words of Psalm 95—have been the opening psalm of invitation to morning prayer for the faithful for six thousand years. Similarly, the words of Psalm 121—"We lift our eyes to the hills, from where does our help come?"—have called the faithful to prayer as the day draws to a close for just as long. One can find the venite referred to by other names as well, such as "opening psalm." A psalm by any other name is still a rose.

Next, a *collect* for the day or the season or the hour itself is said, sometimes all three. A collect is a formal prayer that sort of collects or gathers us all up, one might say. "Deliver us, Almighty God, from the service of self alone that we may do the work you have given us to do, in truth and beauty and for the common good; for the sake of the One who comes among us as one who serves . . . " are the words of one of the collects used as the workday begins. Saying these ancient collects binds us to one another and to the whole community of saints.

A *canticle*, or hymn of praise, follows the collect. These ancient hymns taken from Scripture are associated with certain parts of the day and with certain offices. Simeon's Song, for example, from the gospel of Luke—"Lord, now let your servant depart in peace as you have promised, for with mine own eyes I have seen the Savior"—has been sung or said at the end of the day since early Christian times. It is a way of gently reminding—calling us, even—to daily seek the One who comes in the daily rounds of our lives.

Then the *psalm* (or *psalms*) *appointed* for the day are read. The praying of the Psalter is one of the oldest parts of the practice of the daily office. It is, in some ways, the core of the entire discipline, which is why the Psalter is often referred to as the prayer book of the Bible.

Depending on the community, the number of psalms said in each office or in each day will vary. In some monastic communities, the entire Psalter is sung or said each day or each week. In most contemporary versions of the office, the Psalter is arranged in a thirty-day cycle, so that the psalms are prayed through each month.

It is also often the case that individual psalms have been shortened to make them easier to sing or say or to make them more conducive to prayer. We still see the remnants of such in the responsive readings sections of many contemporary hymnals. By the way, when we are talking about these ancient traditions of prayer, *contemporary* is a word one uses for anything fewer than a couple of hundred years old.

The *reading of Scripture* comes next. Each day, lessons from the Old Testament, the New Testament, and the Gospels are read. The pattern and the cycle of readings vary, but the intent is the same: to root our worship and our prayer in the Word of God. The most commonly used pattern for determining the cycle of Scripture readings for each day follows the Common

Lectionary, but other arrangements for reading the Scriptures through each year or two are appropriate as well.

The Scripture reading is followed by a *response to the Word*. In some breviaries this takes the form of silence. In others, one of the creeds is recited. In yet others, another hymn of praise is sung. Some people, especially when saying the office alone, choose to use this moment for meditation or journaling the Scriptures.

Then come the *prayers of the people*, in which prayers of thanksgiving, intercession, and petition are offered. Most versions of the office have collects that are used to guide one through such things, with pauses for names to be said aloud or "in the secrets of our heart," as one of my favorite prayer books says. They also gently guide us to include the whole world in our prayers and not just our immediate circle of family and friends.

During at least one of the offices each day, there is a *confession of sin*. It concludes with saying the *Our Father* and, sometimes, with a collect.

A *blessing* brings the office to a close. "Thanks be to God," we say as we are sent forth to seek Christ and to serve the kingdom and to be the body of Christ in this world on this day.

This basic shape or frame—versicle, venite, collects, canticle, Psalter, Scripture, response, prayers of the people, blessing—is found in all forms of the office, no matter which prayer book from which community one uses.

Which leads to the next adventure—finding a prayer book to use.

Some of us grew up in a tradition where the liturgy of the hours was part of the ongoing life of the community. Even if you did not participate, you at least knew where to turn when you began to be drawn to practice this ancient discipline.

But for some of us, being drawn to the daily office means that another search is about to begin. Sometimes people will tell me that they would like to participate in this ancient way of prayer. "Which of the scores of prayer books should I use?" they ask me. "Which set of prayers should I pray?"

I tell them what I can.

Some prayer books are large, elaborate affairs. They have names like the *Daily Office Book, St. Joseph's Missal,* or the Book of Common Prayer. They not only contain the basic prayers of the offices themselves—the versicles and collects and canticles and so forth—but they also contain the lectionary scriptures so that you only need the one book to say the day's prayers. Otherwise, you have to use a prayer book and a Bible. Which is not a bad thing, of course, but it can be difficult in some settings.

It is generally easy to tell that you have one of these prayer books in your hands. They weigh about as much as a small child and cost a pretty penny and generally have a lot of ribbons in them. It is also virtually impossible to pretend that these prayer books are anything other than religious books of some sort. Which is fine if you are only going to use it in private, but it can be a little unsettling if you are going to say your office in the lunchroom down the hall, and you would rather that no one knew what you are up to. *Stealth prayer* is the ancient term for that, by the way.

I also should say, in the category of being honest with you, that the prayer books issued by any group—Franciscans or Catholics, the Greek Orthodox or Benedictines of one sort or another, and any other large group, for that matter—carry within them something that makes them both a wonderful personal prayer book and a bear to work your way through as a personal prayer book. These books are made for corporate worship, not private worship.

The reality is that most of us who say this prayer will do so in private most of the time. There are some tricks you will need to wrestle through if you are going to take a corporate prayer book and pray it by yourself. For example, you have to be able to navigate your way around a lectionary without the aid of a priest or officiant, the people who seem to have been given the secret code that cracks the lectionary listings.

You also have to have some knowledge of the liturgical calendar, and which days are feast days and which ones are fast days and which days are days of special devotion, but not so special that they have their own collects. It can be some combination of confusing and intimidating and discouraging, none of which is really very helpful to someone who is just beginning this practice.

Another thing that happens is that you find yourself waiting on the leader to say his line so you can say the next one. Except that there is no leader. Not to mention the places where you do not know whether it is appropriate to say, "The Lord be with you," if there is no one with you to answer back, or exactly whether you are qualified to pronounce your own absolution following the confession of your own sins.

One can use such a corporate prayer book for personal prayer, but frankly, it takes some courage and confidence and knowledge and experience to be comfortable doing so. I have seen people throw up their hands at the notion of trying to say morning prayer on their own using such a book.

If you are just starting out in praying the daily office, it may be wise to pick another prayer book as a companion. If not, you can find yourself so confused and discouraged just trying to figure out what to say when that you give up the practice before it has a chance to take root in your life.

I also recommend that you do not buy your first pair of running shoes on Monday and sign up for a marathon on the following Saturday.

There is a second set of books one can use to begin to pray the daily office. For a lot of reasons—the growing sense that our prayer lives as individuals and as the Church are not as deep as they might be, the longing for connection to the deeper traditions of the Church, the conviction that we need some sort of rule for sacrifice and discipline in our spiritual lives, the same sorts of reasons that drew you to this book, in fact—for all these reasons and more, there has been an interesting pile of books published in the last few years that seek to make the office more accessible to individuals who are just discovering it and who pray alone. They range from books like *The Divine Hours* by Phyllis Tickle, which is a new version of the ancient Orthodox tradition, to readers that are more contemplative in nature, like Reuben Job's *A Guide to Prayer.*

These prayer books are designed for people who are just taking their first steps into fixed-hour prayer. These prayers are laid out more simply and have fewer secret codes. They are not corporate prayer books, so they do not require you to keep changing pronouns in your head as you pray. They are made for saying this most corporate of prayer in private.

By necessity, some of these books are large because they carry one throughout the year, so they can be a little cumbersome. But they often look like ordinary books, if stealth prayer is part of what you aim to practice.

Some people get nervous at the idea of a writer somewhere just making up his or her own prayer book. The folks who get the most nervous are the people who make them. I know this because I have worked on two of them myself.

One of my friends was working on a breviary at the same time I was working on one, and we would see each other twice a year or so. Whenever we met during that time, we would throw our arms around each other in gratitude that neither of us had been struck by lightning for doing such an audacious thing.

A third way to begin the daily office is to use what I call the Little Office of Saint Somebody. These prayers have generally been taken from the breviaries used by the folks who gathered around a particular monastic community. *The Little Book of the Hours,* from the Community of the Little Brothers and Sisters of Jesus, and *Saint Benedict's Prayer Book for Beginners* are a couple of examples. They are a good place for beginners or for people who are looking to refresh their practice of the daily office by setting aside their regular books for a season or so. Like during Lent or Advent, for example.

These prayer books will generally fit into your pocket or your purse, and they contain a cycle of daily prayer for a couple of weeks or a month or so. Their brevity and simplicity lend themselves readily to the formation of the habit, which is about as mundane a way to talk about such a marvelous thing as one can get. Those who begin with such books are often drawn to more complex books as time goes by.

The fourth kind of prayer book is my favorite, though hard to find. They are books that are made by hand, by some soul who was mysteriously drawn to the mystery of this prayer.

Someone dug through books and photocopied prayers from this place and that one, typed them in or scribbled them out, careful to be sure they followed the form and the shape and the intent of the traditional offices. Then they cut them up and pasted them into a little book or onto cards that they carried in their pockets or their journals or their Bibles. As time went by, they would hear or learn or see some new bit of the practice—discover the canticles or decide to paraphrase their own psalter or stumble on collects they had never seen before—and they would add or subtract or change or adapt their daily prayers.

I call them the little breviaries of Saint Whatever Your Name Is. They are the most breathtaking prayer books of all to me. Whenever I get to see one, I just want to lie down and catch my breath. They are also the way that many of us who share this prayer actually began.

Very often, a person I am talking to about praying the daily office will ask, "Where do I go to find such things?"

For those who are not used to praying the daily office, the search for a prayer book will require a field trip to some places you never thought you would go. If you have been following Jesus for any length of time, you should be used to this by now.

You may well need to speak with a priest or a minister from a tradition that is more liturgical than the one you are a part of.

One can very often find such books at a retreat center run by liturgical traditions as well. Catholic bookstores and the bookshops found in Episcopal cathedrals and parishes are places where you can find such books and hold them in your hands and thumb through them.

If you are going to respond to this call to prayer, you will eventually have to choose a prayer book to use for the daily office. Here is the golden rule for choosing which set of prayers you are going to say: pick a set of prayers you like, and begin to pray them. If you are drawn to participate in "the very prayer which Christ Himself, together with His body, addresses to the Father," then there is only one way to go wrong, and that is not to begin.

The particular version, the set of prayers you pray, is up to you. And how many offices—seven or four or two—and which of the offices you will say—morning or noon or evening or night—those choices are up to you as well. The One who has drawn you to begin will guide you as you go along.

"If you ask for bread, will you get a stone? How much more then can you trust your heavenly Father?" Those words from the Son of God suggest to me that God's answer to the petition "O Lord, open our lips" is not likely to be, "I am sorry; you picked the wrong prayer book, and you are saying them seventeen minutes too late each day."

Pick a set of prayers and begin. If we can be trusted to work out our own salvation with fear and trembling, as Saint Paul once wrote that we must, we can probably be trusted to pick out a prayer book.

4

PRAYING UPSIDE DOWN

Let yourselves be built, as living stones, into a spiritual temple for the holy work of offering spiritual sacrifices acceptable to God.
—Saint Peter

The surrendering of ourselves to a life hidden in Christ . . . can be nothing other than the participation of our whole being in the work of God.
—The Rule of Taizé

What the church does, first and foremost, is worship the living God. It is out of our common worship that our understanding of God proceeds.
—Jeffrey Lee

FOR MOST OF MY GROWING-UP YEARS, MY FATHER'S FATHER lived next door to us. Or, I should say, we lived next door to him. Pop was there first.

His face and hands were worn by the sun, from all the years he had spent working in his yard. He had lost enough of his hair that he looked to be adorned with a monk's tonsure, and the gray hair that was left was wild and unruly.

Pop was a small man. I used to love to stand next to him, because he was one of the few people on the planet I have ever towered over. He had this way of looking at you where he would crane his neck around and up and sort of look past you with one eye and stare at you with his other one.

Not only did we live on the same big piece of property with him, but we went to the same church. It was the church his father had helped to start, the church where my father grew up, the church where my folks got married, and the church where my grandfather was the song leader. It was the place where some very good and fine someones first "told me the Story and showed me its ways," as the words of the old prayer go.

About once a month or so, Pop would take us all out to lunch after church on Sunday. It was generally good fun to go to lunch with Pop. For one thing, he brought my grandmother, whom I dearly loved. The only bad part about Sunday lunch with my grandfather was question time. It was always the same question, and I always dreaded it.

First he would cock his head around and get me in his sights. "Boy," he would then say, "what did you get out of the service today?"

I was a teenager, and most Sundays what I got out of the service from up in the balcony where I sat with all of my friends was very different from what he got out of the service up on the chancel in the song leader's chair or in the front row, where he sat for years after hanging up his song leader's hat. In about eight years of Sunday lunches, I do not think I ever got the right answer, not as far as he was concerned. It bugged me to death. I was one of those very eager and likely very annoying kids who sat in the first row at school and who always had their hand up from Monday through Friday because they knew the answer to the teacher's question. It made me crazy not to know the right answer when my grandfather asked me the Sunday question.

Years later, I was having a conversation with a pastor of a far more liturgical church than the one I was raised in. The pastor was telling me about Bill, a man in the church who was complaining about so much liturgy being used in the service on Sunday. It was more formality than he was generally used to. I had been going there for some time, and I wondered about the same things Bill was wondering about too, though I was falling in love with the liturgy in those days.

"I do not like all the rigmarole," Bill said. "I don't get it. Just sing a couple of the good old songs, and then preach me a good sermon, and let's go home."

"The liturgy is not for you, Bill," the pastor told him. "It is for God. On Sunday, our job is to put on the best possible show for God that we know how to do. We are doing so in the way that God's people have always done it. If you get something out of it, Bill, that's fine. But if you do not, then that is okay too. It isn't even for you."

Sometimes now, I will talk to a friend somewhere who is thinking about changing churches. And sometimes one of them will say that he changed places because he was not getting anything out of the sermons anymore. Or the way the services were being conducted "just wasn't doing it for me anymore." Sometimes when I talk to people about the daily office, they say the same sorts of things.

All these years later, I finally have a good answer for my grandfather's Sunday question.

"Boy, what did you get out of the service today?"

"It was not even for me," I wish I had known to say.

Our life with God and our hunger for a deeper, richer, ongoing life in communion with God demands that we be able to hold in tension things that often seem to be contradictory. Any attempt to be with God, whether in the course of our prayer and worship or in the course of our daily lives, has to be lived in the light of some sense of paradox.

God is within us and God is without us. Jesus is with us, and Jesus has ascended into heaven. The kingdom has come, and the kingdom is still to come. We have been saved, and we have yet to be judged. These are the paradoxes of our life with God.

The paradox of worship is this: we perform these acts of worship, but they are not actually for us. We do these things for God, and then we are the ones who are changed.

We offer our songs of praise, and we are the ones who are moved to joy. We offer our thanksgivings, and we are the ones who are blessed by them. We offer the ancient prayers of the psalms, and we are the ones who begin to hear "the prayer of God that rises in our hearts," as my friend Father Edward Farrell says. We offer the gifts of bread and wine in the Eucharist, and we are the ones who are fed and strengthened.

"Experience has taught the race," wrote Annie Dillard, "that these habits of life are not the means but the conditions in which the means operates. You do not have to do these things, not at all . . . unless you want to know God. They work on you, not him."

But they work on no one if we do not do them at all. And they may not work on us the way that they might, if we simply do them for ourselves, for our own edification and entertainment, or for our own spiritual growth, even. Worship is not really about us.

The practice of praying the daily office has within it the same sort of profound paradox that is found in the worship we offer each Sunday when we gather to offer whatever it is that we offer to God in the name of worship. Whether we offer our worship with a lot of liturgy and ceremony and ancient "rigmarole," as Bill might say, or whether we offer it with praise choruses and hymn lyrics projected on the walls and newfangled rigmarole.

There is another paradox that I have noticed about us and our life with God. Very often our prayers are for us as well. We spend a great deal of time and energy telling God all of the things we profess to believe that God already knows and is already working on in our behalf, in ways far better than we can desire or pray for, as the old prayer says it. Those prayers are for us. The prayer of the office is for God.

I have spent a fair amount of time during the last twenty years or so reading about and studying monastic traditions. Somewhere it occurred to me that if I wanted to know something about prayer, I might turn to the crowd of folks for whom prayer has been a way of life for a while—say, fifteen centuries or so. There is a chance they may know something.

It seems reasonable to me. If you want to learn how to use your computer, you ask someone who uses one. If you want to learn to pray, you turn to people who pray.

So I visited their monasteries and read their books, the few of them that have been written, comparatively speaking. As Emilie Griffin wrote, "People who pray, really pray, do not talk about it much." (If you would like to work on your humility, read that sentence every day for two years while you write a book about prayer.)

I am searching for the wisdom about the life of prayer that can be transposed into the life of a person who is called to pray without ceasing without the benefit of living in a community that exists to do just that.

Some of my favorite books are the *regula*, little books that are like operators' manuals for monks and nuns. *Regula* is a word that means "rule." "It is called a regula," wrote Saint Benedict in his preface to the Rule of Saint Benedict, "because it regulates the lives of those who live by it."

Some of the things I read in such rules have nothing to do with me and my life, because I am not a monk. Some of the things in them have to do with proscribing the behaviors and habits of people who live in that particular setting, and it simply does not help me with the way I live in today's world. For example, there are very few instances where taxes and iPods and teenagers and ultimate driving machines are specifically mentioned in the Rule of Saint Benedict.

But some of what is to be found there can be transposed into our lives here; one just has to change some pronouns or flip some stuff on its head to see what is underneath it. Which is what we poets are on the planet to do in the first place.

Some years ago I stumbled onto a copy of the Rule of Taizé, written by the founder of the community. Brother Roger's community in France is widely known for their music and for worship services that are often conducted "in the Taizé tradition," with silence and candlelight and soft music. I love it when one of my younger friends invites me to this "new" way of worshiping, as though candles and silence and chants have just been invented.

I was cruising along in the Rule of Taizé and stumbled onto a sentence that caught my attention and still does. "Corporate prayer," wrote Brother Roger to his monks, "does not dispense us from personal prayer. The one sustains the other."

I am reading between the lines here, but evidently, if you live in Brother Roger's community, a community that is specifically built around the work of saying the corporate daily prayer of the faithful, then you have to guard against your prayer being so caught up in the corporate prayer of the Church that you neglect your ongoing personal prayer, your ongoing dialogue with Christ.

This is not the problem I have, and I may not be alone. I am a card-carrying member of the Me Generation. Personal prayer is not one of the things I struggle with. But if you flip over the line Brother Roger wrote and bring it outside the walls of the community in which he lives and into the world in which we live, it comes out this way: Personal prayer does not dispense us from corporate prayer. The one sustains the other.

Personal prayer to a personal Savior does not excuse us from our responsibility to participate in corporate prayer, in the ancient tradition that is to be prayed by us all to the One who made us all.

I am not about to theologically thumb my nose at the wonder of the fact that the One who made us personally entered our world and seeks to come and be with me personally—so that I might dwell in him and he in me. But I hasten to remind us both that we live with the paradox of the God within and the God without, the One who made us and the One who comes among us.

And I have a sense that the One who made us is not actually my personal God.

I made a sort of technological breakthrough recently. I would not say I went so far as to move into the twenty-first century, but even those of us who are confirmed Luddites make a little progress from time to time.

We bought an iPod. An iPod nano, to be exact, for those of you who know about such things. And a little speaker thingy—I am still learning some of the technical terms—that you plug the iPod into and get music all through the house. I also got some personal speaker thingies I can plug in my ears and use whenever and wherever I want, save maybe when I am strapped into my seat during takeoff or in the second pew at the cathedral where I worship.

Of course, I had to get my younger and savvier neighbor to come and show me how to use it. I would not have bothered him, except that my children have moved out now, and I have no one else to turn to when it is time to figure out how to make my computer do something that the man who sold it to me promised I could do very easily.

So now I have a way to personally program my own personal soundtrack for my own personal life.

We live in the age of the personal, I think. At least, I like saying it that way better than I like referring to myself as a member of the Me Generation.

We have personal soundtracks on portable personal sound systems so we can sort of clear out our own personal space whenever we happen to be out there among the human race.

We have personal computers, and we can hire personal shoppers—though I have to confess that I am still personally up to the task of disposing of my personal income myself. We have personal identification numbers, and some of us have personalized license plates.

I heard on the radio an advertisement that says I have a personal banker, though we have never actually met. And if you met me, you could tell by looking at me that I clearly have personal style that fits comfortably around my persona.

Once a quarter, I get a personal invitation in the mail to have my car's oil changed and engine belts checked by my personal mechanic, the one who works for the dealership that services my ultimate personal driving machine. Actually, my car was made in Germany for someone else in 1986; it says so in my mechanic's personal files that he keeps on the personal driving habits of all of the persons who have ever owned this car.

I take personal responsibility whenever I should, or at least when I have to, and I am personally convinced that I am on the planet to be my own person.

So it is not really a surprise that my personal prayer to my personal Savior is all too often about one person.

We live in the age of the personal. And personally, I am tired of it.

Sometimes it seems we have convinced ourselves that even though we are expecting God to work in mysterious ways on our behalf, our call to offer praise and worship to the One who made us is the sort of thing that can be taken care of once a week in an hour or so between the Sunday school hour and the Sunday buffet.

The call that comes to us from the tradition of the daily office, the call that comes to us from the untold millions of the faithful who went before us, suggests something else altogether. It suggests that we are to worship God as much as we are to petition God.

In a few weeks, the rakes we own will make their first appearance of the spring in our yard. It will not be too long before the mulch will be delivered. Here we go again.

Sometime soon, I have to rake off all of the winter mulch, rake up all of the leaves that have ended up in my yard over the winter, turn over the dirt in all of the flower beds, and reset some of the bricks in the patio and the walkways that have been dislodged by the winter rains. I have to prune the roses and trim the hedges and cut back the monkey grass, fix the gate in the back fence, reset the hinges and the lock on the front gate, power-wash the porch, put a new screen in the doors to my studio, edge the patio, put pine straw in the lower garden, and figure out a way to attach a rosebush to the house, the one that is so big now it keeps falling over and blocking the front gate.

None of which I can actually do in a weekend. So I have some yard work to do, every day for weeks to come. And the truth is that the yard is not going to look like much for some weeks to come yet.

There is a moment out there somewhere, though, a single afternoon or evening, when I will come around the corner, and the roses will have begun to bloom or the light will fall just right on the fountain, or I will see the cardinals playing tag in the hedges, and it will take my breath away.

The next day, of course, I will have to weed the flower beds or mow the little bit of lawn that I have not yet managed to eliminate. Some folks like having big lawns to mow. I like my lawn cut into small sections and stacked on a truck and hauled away to make room for things that do not have to be mowed each weekend.

Between now and the time we will put the garden to bed next winter, I figure I have about twelve moments of magic coming, and I could miss some of them if I do not do the daily work it takes to make such moments possible. I also think it is worth every moment of work for those six or eight or twelve moments of pleasure, whenever they come and whatever they turn out to be like when they take my breath away.

One of the reasons it's hard for us to say the daily office is that on most days, prayer is more like weeding a flower bed for the third time this month than it is some divine and mystical experience. The truth is that for most of the time—for all time, according to the ones that have gone before us—the office has a kind of mundane, everyday sort of feeling. There is a blessed ordinariness to it. The daily office is not called *daily* for nothing, you know.

There is a temptation for all of us to feel as though worship is not really worth much unless we are personally moved by it.

If we are not somehow emotionally touched, then our worship does not seem spiritual to us. It helps to remember that liturgy is the work of the people, not the magic wand of God.

To say the office is to say that I am going to keep doing my chores. I am going to keep raking the leaves or mowing the grass or pulling up the weeds, even if it is a long time until the roses bloom. I will keep saying these psalms until the prayer of God rises in my heart. I will offer my thanksgivings even when I am not very thankful. I will offer my prayer and praise on the days when I am tired or distracted or busy or lost. This sacrifice of praise and thanksgiving is not only reasonable, but in the end, it may even make me lively somehow. Maybe even fully alive.

Sometimes it is hard to persevere in saying the office, because there is no immediate sense that anything is happening when we do. I only know this: if you want some roses to bloom, then you have to do some raking and some mulching and some weeding and some pruning and some waiting. I also know that some evening in May, when I come around the corner at dusk to check to see if the front gate is locked for the night, the breeze will be just right, and I will be paying attention enough to smell them, and the moment will be as holy as any prayer that ever rose as incense to the One who made us.

From time to time, something fine may well happen to me while I am saying the morning or evening prayer. But not if I do not make my office with great care, my "daily offering of fresh flowers to the Beloved Spouse," as Charles de Foucauld once put it. Not if I do not say my prayers.

It is not easy to say the prayers when nothing much seems to come from it each day. Is that really a good reason not to do the work of God?

Personal prayer does not dispense us from corporate prayer. The one sustains the other. Our ongoing conversation with Christ does not excuse us from the call to share in the ongoing praise and worship that is to be offered up by the body of Christ.

The prayer of the office can teach me that the world of prayer is much larger than just my own sweet personal self. I may well discover that prayer is not actually even for me.

If I say the words of the divine office often enough and carefully enough and faithfully enough, I may well find a pearl of great price.

Here is the pearl: the world is not my personal oyster.

5

THE DIVINE OF THE DAILY OFFICE

Sing and make music to the Lord in your hearts,
and give thanks every day for everything.
—SAINT PAUL

In the regularity of the office, the love of Jesus
springs up within us, we know not how.
—THE RULE OF TAIZÉ

The Divine Hours are prayers of praise offered as a sacrifice
of thanksgiving and faith to God. . . . To offer them . . .
is to assume the "office" of attendant upon the Divine.
—PHYLLIS TICKLE

I TRY NOT TO WRITE SENTENCES WITH BIG THEOLOGICAL words in them very often. Those kinds of words scare me when other people use them; they really scare me when I do. I am a poet, not a theologian. Wonderer is about as high as I can go.

I try not to write pages with big prophetic-sounding sentences very often either. And pronouncements are things I generally avoid like the plague, no matter who makes them. High-toned pronouncements are for the professionals, I think, so I try not to engage in such at home or in public.

But here comes a pronouncement or two. Know that I am working out these sentences with the same amount of fear and trembling that I am continuing to work out my salvation. I will speak as softly as I can and try to sneak them up on you.

Our modern Church has some distinct advantages over the early Church. Or at least I suspect it does. We have better youth programs and better acoustics and finer buildings. We have better literature that is more easily available to our flocks, most of whom happen to be literate. We have some pretty fair preachers, or at least we have some who are more fun to listen to than the blessed Saint Augustine. (Have you ever actually attempted to read Saint Augustine?)

We have better choirs, I suspect, and we can put on a Sunday morning service with more art and more dignity and more beauty than ever before. We have mailing lists and newsletters and Web sites. We have educational buildings and discipleship classes and Bible study groups where students bring their own Bibles. We have Sunday school buses and youth lock-ins and Christian rock-and-roll bands.

What we do not have so much of sometimes, it seems to me, is the depth of spirit and of devotion and of piety—now, there is a scary word—that marked the life of the faithful in the hundreds and thousands of years before us, the centuries that produced the Church we built our buildings and programs around in the first place.

It is worth noting, I believe, that this tradition of daily prayer is one of the practices our modern Church does not do that the ancient Church did. We preach sermons, study the Scriptures, gather to worship on the Sabbath, teach our children the faith, and fellowship with one another—but we do not say our prayers.

Sometimes it occurs to me that I am a member of the first generation of followers of Yahweh in six thousand years for whom the offering of daily fixed-hour worship and praise and prayer—a tradition practiced and treasured and passed down to us from the Hebrews to the apostles to the early Christians to the fathers and mothers of the faith who sustained this Church we now call home—is no longer deemed a necessity or an obligation or a duty or even an opportunity.

Sometimes when I think of that, I want to fall on my knees and maybe even on my face.

We who will get up and walk, or even run miles in the mornings, not to mention those of us who are not willing to wait for there to be enough light to see the bottom of the flag or for the frost to go away before we tee off; we who will haul ourselves through our neighborhoods in the dark to make sure that we have the box scores as quick as we can—for all kinds of reasons, including some good ones, I suppose, we will not, cannot, do not rise in the morning to greet the dawn with a song of praise on our lips, as did those who went before us.

We who will stay up late to watch the televised version of the news that we heard on our drive home at six, who will TiVo enough must-see television that we have to stay up late to keep up, who will not go to sleep without reading a novel, who will burn the candle at both ends and in the middle if we can figure how to get it lit, will not end our days with praise and worship and confession and blessing.

We will not do these things in the name of love or discipline, devotion or worship. We will not even do it for selfish reasons, or even as a reliable way of self-actualization, to put it in its least-favorable context—which, in our Western American, twenty-first-century, self-help, and consumer-driven culture, is astonishing. And that includes some of us in certain communities of faith who made a promise to pray the office when we joined. Some of us did not even notice the promise we made at our confirmation, and the clergy do not point it out very often.

And if you believe the scholars and the media and the pundits who predict our increasing collective future irrelevance, then I am also a member of the generation that will preside over the death of the Church. Call it postmodern, call it post-Christian, call it Post Toasties if you want to, but there is a world out there that says we—the Church united, divided, militant, or otherwise—can do nothing to spread the gospel here on earth. Much less do anything to make each hour of the day or night any holier.

The witness of those who went before us is that we can. We just don't.

We very often say to one another that we are the body of Christ. The Scriptures have taught us that, and so have all those who went before us. And we say it with some degree of certainty and hope and some sense of humility and obligation. We remind ourselves that if Christ is to be seen in this world today, it will be because we have answered the call to be the hands and the feet of Christ. We remember that it will be because we have answered the call to feed the poor and seek the lost and visit the prisoners. And we are right to think those things, as long as we do so with humility and with love and with fear and with trembling.

But we who claim to be Christ's body would do well to remember the way of prayer of those who went before us, the ones who built the Church. *The Encyclopedia of the Catholic Church* says, "By tradition going back to early Christian times, the divine office is devised so that the whole course of the day and night is made holy. . . . It is the very prayer which Christ Himself, together with His body, addresses to the Father."

If we are the body of Christ, then we are to offer the very prayer which Christ himself, together with his body—with his hands and feet and knees and eyes and voice, all of those things we profess to be called to be and sometimes by the grace of God actually are—addresses to the Father.

Why is it that this seems like news to us?

We are not all called to be monastics. We are not all called to be teachers or prophets or apostles or administrators within the body of Christ, according to Paul. But the prayers were never meant to be just for monastics anyway; they were for all the people of God, people like you and me. And evidently for people like Peter and Paul and Silas, according to the stories in Acts.

Paul is the one some folks quote when they tell you that Jesus came to free us from the law, and therefore from the ancient liturgy. But look at the stories in Acts and the writings of the early Church. Paul evidently wrote a fair number of his letters in between trips to gather with others to say the daily prayers.

We are, according to Paul, all called to pray without ceasing. And according to the story and the history and the tradition of those who went before us, those whose faith and devotion and practice were based on the work of the founders of the Church, we have all been given the prayers that will allow us to do just that. This way of prayer was part and parcel of the life of the early Church. Jesus may have freed us from the law, but I am not sure he meant to free us from worship of the One who made us.

It occurs to me that if this way of prayer was good enough for the faithful to pray while waiting for the Messiah to come— alongside Moses and David and Jeremiah and the rest, if it was good enough for Jesus himself to have prayed when he was a young man, and if it was good enough for Paul and Peter and James and John, good enough for Abba Antony and Abba Theodore and Abba Pachomius in the desert, good enough for Saint Benedict and Saint Francis and Saint Hildegard and Saint Teresa, good enough for John Wesley and Martin Luther and Thomas Cranmer, it may well be good enough for me. Perhaps a little old-time religion might do me some good.

Of course, I personally would rather just talk to God when I want to, remind God of the things that personally matter to me the most, and then get on with the real world as I think I personally know it to be as quickly as I can.

I suspect that I am not alone.

I mentioned to you before that I am not a scholar. To my credit, so to speak, I attended classes and dropped out of some very highly respected and nationally known private religious liberal arts institutions. One still sends me letters to the attention of "Dear Alumnus," though I did not receive a diploma there or anywhere else.

I went to college to study English literature. I was raised in a family of writers and publishers and artists and painters, around singers and musicians and performers, all of whom encouraged me when I said I wanted to become a writer. So I did not go to college to figure out what I wanted to do. When the time came, I packed up my VW convertible, stopped on the way out of town to buy a copy of *Sweet Baby James* as my parting gift to myself, and headed off to study English literature. After a couple of years, I began to work in the family publishing business.

Some people go to school on work-study programs. I was on the stealth-study program. I would register at a school, pay the bill, sign up for two or three English lit classes, and then drop out and move to another school at almost precisely the moment that the registrar's office would complete their paperwork and discover I had not taken freshman chemistry or attended chapel often enough and write me a note to say that I could not actually attend classes there. By then, I had already taken the three classes I wanted to take at that particular school and was ready to move on.

Most schools barely noticed that I was there or that I left early. The secret to the stealth-study program is to register late and pay cash and never live in on-campus housing, by the way.

One fall I registered at a school, and two weeks later I got a call from the man who ran the music business program. Unaware that I had just registered for classes there, he offered me an adjunct teaching position in a seminar series. I decided that when colleges were hiring me to lecture, then my student days were over.

Nobody told me that in the history of the planet, fewer than 1 percent of the people who write books for a living actually make a living writing books. Everyone else has to teach or some such thing in order to put food on the table. Teaching positions are hard to come by for college dropouts.

And nobody told me that the family business was going to be sold, and I was going to be out of a job.

And nobody told me that I was not going to be rich and famous.

I tell you that glorious story of my admittedly checkered educational history so I can repeat one of the most common reasons that a lot of us do not participate in this ancient way of prayer: nobody told me. It is one of the things many of us can honestly say when we give reasons for not saying these prayers. Or at least we could, until just a moment ago.

Nobody told me these prayers had been at the core of the life of the devout for centuries. Nobody told me about their history and their power to shape us. Nobody told me I was supposed to be saying these prayers.

It may have been talked about in an elective-course sort of way somewhere in a church I visited, but as you might expect by my college record, I generally elected to take only what I wanted to.

What if it turns out that there is a sense in which saying these prayers is not elective?

Do not misunderstand me; I do not believe that saying these prayers is about our salvation. Saying these prayers is not about qualifying to be in that number when the saints go marching in or out or wherever it is that we are headed for eternity.

But going to church on Sunday, bringing our kids to church, paying our tithes, feeding the poor, or taking care of orphans in South America are not about salvation either. Those things are about the way we live our lives here, and about whether we do the things that we are given to do to help be sure that Christ, through his body, can actually be seen here on earth at all.

When I say that these prayers are not elective, I mean what if some of us are being drawn to say these prayers not to save ourselves but to save the whole world? Or to save the Church? What if we are being called to help restore this ancient prayer as a way to strengthen and sustain the Church in our time, as it strengthened and sustained the Church in its earliest days?

In the post-Reformation world, as the various reform and renewal movements began to spread across Europe and into the New World, there were great changes in the ways of the Church. Some of what went into those changes were honest and necessary reactions to the excesses of the Catholic Church at the time. Some of what went into the changes wrought by the Reformation has as much to do with shifts in the culture and society and politics as it had to do with the Church. But in some ways, as Phyllis Tickle once observed, in some places "we threw out the baby of the ancient along with the bath water of the Roman."

For those of us who are not Catholic or Orthodox, this is the history of the Church we were often taught: Jesus came, Jesus died, Jesus rose again, and Jesus ascended into heaven. Paul wrote his letters and made his mission trips. The Pilgrims brought religious freedom to America. There was a revival in the 1800s, and the real Church was born. That history is a little like saying that American history is the story of the first Thanksgiving, George Washington, Thomas Jefferson, and

D-Day. Some other stuff went on, other stuff that shaped us, bound us together, and made us one.

But the truncated view of the Church many of us were taught has left us with some questions and some fears about the ancient ways of the Church, the ancient ways that sustained the Church in the first place, the ways that made it possible for there to have been any Church for the Pilgrims to bring over.

One of the obstacles to embracing this way of prayer is our ignorance of and our fear of the ancient, our fear of anything that is too close to the Catholic Church. We are afraid that such prayer will lead us astray somehow, and that such liturgical prayer is dead and lifeless and rote. This is what many of us have been taught.

Some of us are also afraid that whoever taught us to be afraid of the ancient was not actually right about it at all. What I am afraid of is that the ones who went before us, who sustained the Church for the eighteen hundred years before the revival broke out here, may have known something that I do not know. They sustained the Church, not me.

And this prayer is one of the ways that they did so.

"The hardest thing about really seeing and really hearing," wrote Frederick Buechner, "is that then you really have to do something about what you have seen and heard."

For years, "nobody told me" was a fine excuse for my rather sketchy educational career and my poor attempts at being an actual working member of our society. Eventually I had to give up the excuse and admit I knew some of the things that I kept saying no one told me. I knew those things and ignored them.

"Nobody told me" was also a perfectly fine reason for me not to say these prayers. Or at least it used to be.

We have all been called to be the body of Christ. We have all been called to pray the prayer that he prays himself, the prayer that makes each day and hour holy, the prayer that he prays through us. We are all responsible if his prayer is not prayed and if it is not heard by the One who made us all.

We are called to pray the prayer that has been prayed without ceasing by God's faithful for six thousand years. The fact that it is so faintly heard in our time is not a function of its irrelevance; it is a function of our ignorance.

I cannot help myself; here comes a pronouncement. (If it helps any, know that I am whispering when I say this, as I generally do when my fear and trembling has led me to say something like this.)

I am increasingly convinced that if the Church is to live, and actually be alive, one of the reasons, maybe the most important and maybe even the only reason, will be because we have taken up our place in the line of the generations of the faithful who came before us. It will be because we pray the prayer that Christ himself prayed when he walked among us and now longs to pray through us.

It will be because we choose to no longer be among the ones who silence the prayer that Christ, through his body, prays to the Father.

It will be because we make sure that the wave of prayer that sustained the Church for all time does not stop when it is our turn to say it each day. It will be because we answer the ancient call to pray without ceasing.

6

THE REAL CURRENCY
OF OUR AGE

Can you not wait one hour with me?
—Jesus of Nazareth

*On hearing the signal for an hour of prayer, we immediately
set aside what we have in hand and go with utmost speed,
yet with gravity and without giving occasion for frivolity.
Indeed, nothing is to be preferred to the Work of God.*
—The Rule of Saint Benedict

*Liturgical time is essentially poetic time, oriented toward
process rather than productivity, willing to wait attentively
in stillness rather than always "pushing" to get the job done.*
—Kathleen Norris

To paraphrase a film critic I once read, an artist lives his life somewhere between the marvelous and the mundane. It is true of most of us, in fact, or at least I believe it is. It is also true of people who pray the daily office. Maybe a better way to say it is that they live their lives somewhere between the daily and the divine. We all do, I suppose.

When it comes to the daily of our lives, some folks are neat and tidy, and others are less so. Some folks plan things out very meticulously, and some folks sort of wing it. Some folks do work that has a fair amount of schedule and predictability; others are kind of making up their lives as they go along. But to greater or lesser degrees, depending on our personalities and the shape of our lives, we plan the things that need to be done in order to live them.

We have Filofaxes and Palm Pilots. We make grocery lists and honey-do lists. We set our alarm clocks, and we program our TiVos. We have automatic deposit and automatic draft, and we make sure we are planning for that glorious day when our children grow up and go off to college or go off to somewhere else (anywhere, if need be). If we are going to move, we do our homework before we buy a house; if we are going to travel, we sort through Priceline; if we are working toward some big event at the holidays, we put a checklist on the refrigerator.

We would not dream of trying to do anything in our lives that really matters to us, whether it is large or small, without making a list or two or twenty-seven, and checking it twice a day.

I have noticed a curious phenomenon. One of the few things that we are reluctant to make lists about and do research about and have a row of boxes to tick off about are the things that have to do with our spiritual lives. I don't know why this is.

We say that our spiritual life is important to us. Sometimes we will even go so far as to say that it is the part of our lives that is the most important to us. We also say, at least we say about everything else that matters to us, that if we do not write it down, we will forget to do it. We say that if we are going to make sure something is done and done well, we need to make a plan so nothing gets missed and nothing gets forgotten.

The place we are least likely to make such a plan is when it comes to our spiritual lives. We would not dream of being this way about anything else.

Then we go back to a retreat or some such event a year later and realize we are being drawn to the same things again, and so we make the same promises again to God and to ourselves. Then we go home and do not make a plan again, and we look up one day and realize that we have moved no further along again.

We are unwilling, it sometimes seems to me, to leave anything in our lives to chance except the way that we live out our lives in communion with the One who gave us life in the first place. It seems odd to me.

I have spent enough time over the years writing and talking and retreating and studying and teaching, dare I say it, about and around and over and through and inside and out of the practice of the daily office to know at least this much: to pray the office is to anchor your life of prayer somewhere between the daily and the divine.

It is easy to talk about the divine part of the practice of any sort of prayer—corporate prayer, liturgical prayer, centering prayer, extemporaneous prayer, contemplative prayer, meditative prayer.

To begin with, any sort of prayer is built around the premise that we are in conversation with the God of the universe—the Center of all things, as Thomas Merton once wrote. And if that is not marvelous and wondrous and mystical, then nothing anywhere is marvelous and wondrous and mystical.

A priest or a minister will say, "Let us pray," and we will all just bow our heads as though nothing out of the ordinary was about to take place. What is about to take place is that we are about to presume to talk to the One who made heaven and earth, and presume that we will be heard. "Hear us, good Lord," we say together in one of the liturgies in the cathedral where I worship, and sometimes I want to add, "Good Lord, he might hear us." There is something so astonishing about the whole notion of talking with God that sometimes I just want to lie down for a few minutes and catch my breath. Every once in a while I will hear someone say, "And so I just told God that I needed this or that," and I wonder how it is they are still standing up.

Then when you get to great and lofty phrases, like "praying without ceasing" and praying "the very prayer which Christ Himself, together with His body, addresses to Father," it is almost more than I can get my head around.

I do not know about the poet who lives in you, but the poet who lives in me just wants to raise his hand in the air when he hears such talk. It makes me want to sing or whisper or shout out loud. It gives me goose bumps when I think about being invited into such a world.

Then I have to go to a convention where I feel lost and inconsequential, or I have to leave home and spend a weekend with a crowd who would rather be at a basketball game than on a prayer retreat. Or deadlines loom and other ones stack up behind them, and some of my momentarily orderly ducks get out of line. The poet in me is less inclined to raise his hands and shout glory at such moments. The shouting part comes to mind, of course, but not the glory part. And I am tired and worn and worried and hurried, and gathering myself up to make my office with great care is just one more thing on my list that I cannot get to.

Which brings us to the other part of the life of prayer. Over here, we have the marvelous; over there, we have the mundane. On this hand, the divine; on that one, the daily.

At some point, all of this high-minded discussion about our life of prayer has to work its way into the dailyness of our lives. It has to be stuck in and around and up next to the meetings and the schedules and the packing and the leaving and the coming home of our lives.

At some point, we have to move from talking about prayer to saying our prayers. If the marvelous that is possible in our lives of prayer is to have a chance to appear, it will be because we have done the mundane.

We all go through times when one set of stories from the Gospels or another keeps catching our eye.

One year, the stories of Jesus healing people were just sort of up in my face for months. Another year, I kept listening over and over to the instructions Jesus gave to his disciples about how they were to live once they were on their own. Once I spent the whole year just focusing on questions people asked him. The next year I kept noting the questions Jesus asked them.

During the season of Epiphany, the lectionary takes us through all these great stories of Jesus among us here on earth. One year, the stories that would not leave me alone had punch lines that go like this:

"I know there are a lot of hungry people here on the hill-side. How are we going to feed them?"

"If you want some fish, try the other side of the boat."

"What exactly do you want from me?"

"If somebody takes your coat, he may need your shirt as well."

"I am going to need a ride to Jerusalem for Passover. I need you to go to town and see this guy about a colt."

"Okay, Mother, tell them to bring me the water jars."

"Somebody get practical here; we need a plan."

Jesus did not actually say that last one, of course, but he might have. Maybe some scribe just missed it, as my friend Reuben Welch used to say.

There is another thing I have learned about joining in the prayer that sanctifies the day. There are some real practicalities involved with saying the office. And if you do not deal with those things, then you limit the number of times the divine has a chance to make an appearance within the daily office.

"I am drawn to begin to pray the office," someone will say. "How do I begin?"

That is not a question about the divine; it is a question about the daily. It is exactly the sort of question that makes all the difference.

My friend Father Edward J. Farrell used to say, "The three greatest obstacles to the spiritual life are inertia, amnesia, and mañana." Whenever we set out to do something important to us, we make choices, we make lists, we make schedules. If it matters, we make a plan.

How do you begin to say the office? You begin the same way you begin to do anything else that matters in your life. Ask some questions; take some notes; do some research. Get practical here; make a list.

Jesus would tell you to go to town and see this guy who will be looking for you. Put your net on the other side. If you pressed him, he might tell you that it is going to take some daily to get to the divine.

I have a friend who lives in New Orleans. He is a writer and a speaker, and we have a lot of friends in common. For a time, we were even published at the same house.

So whenever he and I are in the same town at the same time, I make sure that I figure out a way to spend a few minutes with him. It happens most often at the book shows in the summer that he and I both go to in order to attend to the business of being writers. Over the years, I have learned that the best way to get a writer to sit down with you is to offer to buy him a meal, so I call him up and make the offer, and sure enough, he happens to have the lunch hour free.

There have been many times I have discovered that I am one of four or five lunch appointments for him for the day. I do not know who feeds him in August.

"I just have to run to my room for a minute," he said one day at lunch. I knew that he had not been well, and I figured he needed to go and take his medicine or something. So he left the table, and after a minute or so, I remembered a phone call I needed to make, and I went out into the lobby to find a phone.

I rounded the corner and found my friend sitting in a chair in the lobby, with his eyes closed and his hands clasped together. He looked like a thousand other convention goers who were grabbing a quick nap before the next meeting. I watched him for a minute and finally figured out that he was saying his office.

When he came back to the table, I told him that his secret was safe with me. There was no need for a bunch of religious booksellers to know that he was saying his prayers instead of hustling his books.

I think of him sometimes when the bell rings at the church a few blocks away, the bell that rings for prayers. I wonder who is buying him the lunch he is slipping out of now, wherever he may be that day. I wonder what he is working on that he set down for a few minutes while he makes his office with great care. I wonder how long it took to memorize enough of the daily office so that he can say it sitting in a lobby or a plane somewhere. I wonder which office of the day he builds in the time to read the lessons and say the collects and the appointed psalms for the day.

I also wonder what the effect of his living in and out of days that have been made holy by his prayers has had on his work and his community and his sentences and his soul. Though I think I know.

I wonder, too, about the depth of his spirit as opposed to the shallowness of mine. I have wondered about it enough to suspect there is a connection between that depth of spirit and the way that he changed my life all those years ago when I first met him.

And I think, *Why do I not say my office more faithfully?*

Well, it takes too much time to do all of this complicated stuff. The answer is obvious, is it not?

W. H. Auden wrote, "An artist must develop a strict consciousness in regard to time. For we must never forget that we are living in a state of siege." He was not just talking about poets; he was talking about any of us who are trying to live our lives with all the art and love and care we can muster. There is more art in doctoring and schoolteaching and childrearing and all manner of works than most people realize.

I hate saying this in public, but I am going to. There are a lot of days when I just do not have time to say the office. You know how busy we men of letters are.

In the morning, I have to write in my journal and write my six hundred words in whatever new project I am working on. If I do not write in my journal, I forget what has been happening to me. Which is bad enough in and of itself, but it is especially difficult for a guy who makes a living telling stories. If I don't remember my stories, then I have nothing to write the six hundred words about. Eventually I have nothing to write a book about either.

Then I have to get in the car and pick up the day's papers. Then I have to work the crossword. Then I have to do my other writer's work for a while. I have to edit some stuff in the book that I am trying to make something out of from the stuff I ended up with before. I have telephone calls to make and errands to run and letters to write. Sometimes I even have a meeting.

I have four friends with whom I have lunch once a month, cleverly spaced out one per week. On the other days, I stop to eat lunch as well. Then I have to have my nap. And I have to read some stuff that will help me do the work I am trying to do. I have a yard to keep—leaves to rake and beds to weed and mulch to haul and all of those things.

I do have time to take a swim so I can keep my schoolgirl figure. I seem to be able to make tee times and play a round of golf. I have to play golf every week. *Have to* is a relative term, of course, but if you play golf, then you know that "have to play golf" is the proper way to say it. Even if you just live with a golfer, you know that *have to* is the proper term. And the way I play golf, it can take some considerable amount of time to play.

Occasionally there is an interruption of some sort. Like every three hours or so. Which is why we have our plumber and our mechanic and our electrician on speed dial.

I even have friends. The one disadvantage to having friends is that if you are not careful, they will call you or ask you out or drop by the house. Who knew that having friends could be so time-consuming?

I have to eat supper. I have to help clean up the kitchen— okay, I do not have to, but the brownie points that accrue to husbands who cook and clean up, not to mention do the laundry and the yard work, are just too good to pass up.

And did I mention that little armchair in our front parlor, where I like to sit in the evenings? Or that I have to go to bed pretty early, because I get up pretty early. And I have to read for a while before I go to sleep, sometimes for a very long while.

Most days, if it comes right down to it, I simply do not have time to say the office.

And I am fully aware that by most standards my life is not even busy. Most people on the planet live lives that are far busier than mine. I do not have office hours to keep or an office to go to. Other people, people who do actual work that makes an actual contribution to society, have far more demands on their time than I do.

Even so, I just have to say that it is not too difficult for me to make a case that I am too busy to actually have time to participate in "the very prayer which Christ Himself, together with His body, addresses to the Father." This other stuff that I am doing— no matter how great or small, how wonderfully literary or blindingly dull, no matter how long it takes or how little it really matters in any run at all, be it long or short—this other stuff with which I fill up my days is just more important than that.

Why do I not say my prayers?

Well, it takes too much time.

"How we spend our days is how we spend our lives," writes Annie Dillard. "What we are doing with this hour and with that one is what we are doing."

Time is the real currency of our age, and we have to manage our time in relation to our spiritual life as much as we do in relation to any other part of our lives.

Our hearts are where our treasure is, or so we have been told. Our love is where our time goes too. Including the time that some of us say we do not have enough of to spare some to participate in the ancient prayer of God's faithful.

There is some possibility that I am the only one who knows what I am about to tell you. It could be that I am the only one who knows it because I am the only one I know who has taken the time to sit down with the proper equipment and figure it out. Which clearly suggests that writers have too much time on their hands. But it could be that I am simply the only one who will tell you this.

If other people know this, I have never heard anyone say it, and I have never seen it written down anywhere in any of the great spiritual literature written to help us overcome the obstacles to our saying the daily office and participating in the prayer that Christ prays to the Father through his body.

Here it is—it takes about twelve minutes to say an office. If you like, you can read all the scriptures appointed for the day and all the psalms at one office, instead of spreading them out over more than one, and get an office up to some astounding number like seventeen minutes. Or you can spread the scriptures out and average about nine minutes. But what is hard to do is to get an office up to an amount of time that I can reasonably say is too large an amount to have time for on a regular basis.

I may be the only one, but I can spend nine minutes just putting off what I am supposed to be doing for the next sixty minutes. I would be willing to guess that I am not the only one.

It is certainly true that some of my days are more hectic than others, and some of my days are not my own—I am on the road, or a holiday turns up with all of the folks who seem to come with it, or the car breaks down, or the telephone rings. But for me to say that I do not have nine to twelve minutes to say morning prayer is so lame that it is embarrassing to me that I even think it, much less use it as an excuse. It is really embarrassing when I say such a thing about my communion with the One whom I claim to love more than anything or anyone else.

Here is another line that some scribe somewhere may have missed: "Can you not spend twelve minutes with me?"

What, and give up John Stewart and Will Shortz and Patrick O'Brian? And stay up later or get up earlier? Or miss a telephone call and have to call somebody back?

We must never forget that we are living in a state of siege. And we must never forget that, as often as not, we are the enemy at our own gates.

7

LOST BETWEEN THE DAILY AND THE DIVINE

Go into your closet and pray.
—JESUS OF NAZARETH

There will be days when the office is a burden for you.
—THE RULE OF TAIZÉ

*With one concerted voice the giants of the spiritual
life apply the same principle to the whole of life
with the dictum: Discipline is the price of freedom.*
—ELTON TRUEBLOOD

AFTER I HAVE EXHAUSTED THE "I AM TOO BUSY TO SAY the office" section of building a case for not saying the daily office, I move right to the "it is too complicated for me to figure out" argument.

Now, it is not as though I am incapable of handling a fair amount of twenty-first-century stuff. I can do my taxes on Turbo-Tax, and I can look up the box scores from the overnight baseball games on the Internet. I can book airline tickets online too.

I can set up an automatic draft for my mortgage payment, keep the chemical balance right in my swimming pool, and even, wonder of wonders, program TiVo. I can iron a shirt better than all of the women in my life, thank you very much, and I can even watch a Greco-Roman wrestling match and properly keep score. I am not an idiot, no matter what anyone says, including me.

I am licensed to drive a car, and I can balance my own checking account, figure out how to make a living, meet my deadlines, raise my children, be married, own a house, tithe my income, be Jesus to the people on my block, take part in national and local elections, and order whatever I like at a restaurant, even if it is in Italian—all without the daily and hourly supervision of a priest or a minister.

But I have to tell you that moving three ribbons in a prayer book, reading the chart that tells me which lectionary scriptures to read this day or this week, counting back a few Sundays from Easter to see when Lent begins, or knowing which psalms to pray on the eighth day of a thirty-day psalter is too much to ask.

I would really rather just talk to God whenever I want to, say, during commercials when I am driving down the road, carefully enumerating the things that I am counting on God to attend to quickly so that my ducks remain in a row.

I would also really like to be known as a person of prayer as well.

Beyond the time and the complication, we also have to confront the practical questions about the discipline it takes to begin and to sustain such prayer.

People who do not write sometimes think that those who do live in this near-mystical state, furiously scribbling down this great and glorious stuff as it rains down from the heavens. Most writers spend much of their time engaged in the process of tricking themselves into writing anything at all. You thought that we were just tricking our unsuspecting readers into reading it, didn't you? No, no, trickery begins at home. My experience is that a fair amount of the time, I would rather be doing anything on earth rather than writing my six hundred words each day.

I once read about a writer who began his day by retyping everything he had written so far in the story he was working on.

Then, without saying a word to anyone, he would put on his coat and his hat and go out and walk around the block furiously until he thought he knew what came next. Then he would burst in the door to his house, sit down at the typewriter immediately, and begin typing the new sentences in as fast as he could before he outran the burst of new that he seemed to have found on the sidewalk.

Exhausted, and now stymied again, he would take off his coat and hat and repeat the process—retyping the old, walking around the block to find the new, pounding it out furiously until he ran out of new over and over again, or for as many times as he could stand it, and then call it a day.

One day I heard a radio interview with a man who was a consultant and counselor to creative people who were suffering from what people who do not write refer to as writer's block. (Writers are hesitant to say those two words.) He knew about these things because he used to be a writer himself.

He worked with musicians and screenwriters and novelists and such. His advice was this: You do not have to write a book today. You cannot write a book today anyway; there are not enough hours in the day. What you do have to do is to go to work today.

First, go into the room and close the door, he said. Then, before you do anything else or think about anything else, turn on the machine you use to do the work. If it is a fountain pen and paper, take the cap off and go to the spot on the page where you left off. If it is a computer, turn it on and scroll through until you are at the place where you stopped. If it is a piano, put your hands on the keyboard.

Then simply repeat a little bit of what you did the day before. If you are a composer, keep playing those last few bars over and over again. If you are a writer, type in the last few sentences you wrote yesterday.

If you really are an artist, and this is really your calling, he said, then at some moment, two or three minutes perhaps, the work itself—not what you have written, but the physicality of it, the mechanics of it, the process of it, the working—will seize hold of you, and something new will begin to appear. It may be good or bad, it may need more revision or less later on, but the work will take over. You will be working; you will be writing; you will be writing a book.

You do not have to write a book today, he said. You have to go in the room, close the door, start your engines, and move your fingers until the working takes over. The only way to become a writer is to write. If you write enough sentences, you may yet become a writer.

You do not become a person of prayer and then begin to pray. It works the other way around. If you say enough prayers, you may yet become a person of prayer. But you will not become one if you do not pray.

One of the things that will happen if I say the office is this: it can trick me into becoming a person of prayer.

I do not have to become a person of prayer today. I do not have to become pious or devout today. I do not have to become holy today.

"I must say my office with great care," writes Charles de Foucauld. "It is my daily offering of fresh flowers and roses, symbolical of fresh love offered daily to the Beloved Spouse."

What I do have to do today is go into the room and close the door. I have to open up the book. I have to make my offering to the One to whom these prayers are made and the One for whom these prayers are offered. I have to say my six hundred words, if you will, and make my office with great care.

And those days when my office seems like one more chore I would like to avoid? Brother Roger has some advice: "On such days know how to offer your body, since your presence already signifies your desire, momentarily unrealized, to praise your Lord," he writes. "Believe in the presence of Christ within you, even though you feel no tangible response."

I do not know if I will ever become a person of prayer. But I do know that there is only one way it will ever happen.

People of prayer say their prayers—every day.

I like remembering stuff; it is why I write it all down, I suppose. There are all of those golden moments when some grace or wonder came upon us and the memory of it lifts our spirits. I am even okay with the moments of failure and disappointment, the ones that lead us to depend on God truly, as the prayer book calls them. I am okay with such moments precisely because they lead us to depend on God truly.

The problem is that if you remember stuff, then you cannot just remember the good stuff; you have to remember the embarrassing stuff as well.

I am among the most self-conscious, generally nervous, and painfully shy folks I know. Some people are scared of their own shadows. I sent mine away because it kept following me and made me nervous.

It is a wonder to me that I ever go out in public at all. If there is someone who is more afraid of being embarrassed than I am, I am not sure that I want to meet him. I am afraid I would say the wrong thing if I did.

And the number of things about which I am still embarrassed, things that happened long ago, is a very large number. Sometimes I will be somewhere and some object or place will trigger my memory of some moment that was less than one of my finest ones, and then I will be embarrassed all over again.

I am embarrassed that I did not finish college. I am embarrassed about a lot of the things I said to other people back in the days when I was young and in the publishing business and thought that I knew so much more than other folks did.

I am embarrassed that I did not do better for the people who gave me a job once when I was desperate. They were so kind to me, and I treated them pretty shabbily at the end. I am embarrassed about the way I let my father down once or twice in those last years before he passed away.

Even though some of this stuff has been "buried in the deepest sea," as the old song says—and I believe that, really I do—some of it still gives me the willies when I think of it. I believe I have been forgiven; I am just afraid no one has forgotten.

I am sure that there is a name for this. It has to be at least a syndrome if not a full-blown neurosis. I spent three years seeing a therapist, and you would think that I would know what this is called. I was too embarrassed to ask him.

I am embarrassed when I do not make my daily office the way I promised I would. I am especially embarrassed when I do not do so for a longer stretch of time than I am willing to admit to you here.

So from time to time I just hold that embarrassment in my hands and offer it up and giggle. The only thing that I can do is resort to laughing at myself. From time to time, I even begin to believe that the laughter is helpful and may even be holy somehow.

I spent some time in a psych ward once. It was a pretty good, long stretch, in fact, back in the days when folks who were clinically depressed and suicidal got to stay in the hospital long enough to actually get help, rather than just long enough to be told that they are in trouble. They already know they are in trouble; that is why they are there.

Ironically, it happened during the only time in the last twenty years that I was gainfully employed. And I was living in and out of the quasimonastic setting of the Academy for Spiritual Formation at the time too. Somewhere in between working for the Methodists and working with the Rule of St. Benedict, I had a bit of a breakdown.

Unless I thought you really needed it, I would not exactly recommend a few weeks in a psych ward to you, though I would not discourage it either. There is some stuff you do not pay much attention to until some guy takes your shoes and your belt and your car keys away and will not let you have them back until you begin to pay attention to your life and the way that you live it.

I personally would not trade the experience for anything. It is where I learned to grin at myself when I was something less than I meant to be the day before. It is also where I learned to make little boxes.

When I came out of the psych ward, I had this little list of things I had to do each day to help ensure that I did not make a return visit. I had to take my medicine every day, for example, and there was lunch; I had to remember to eat lunch. I got to the psych ward just in time. I was forgetting a lot of things in those days.

So I put these little boxes on the pages of my Filofax—one for the medicine, one for the lunch, one for this, one for that. Whenever I started to feel bad, I could look back through my pages and say something clever, like, "There you go, Ace; you have not been getting your exercise. No wonder." Which does not seem like the sort of system that one would devise in a life-or-death situation, but in the life-or-death situation I was in at the time, it actually worked.

As time has gone along, the boxes have changed, or at least what they have come to represent has changed. My current system, the one that took me all of about twenty minutes this year to scribble on the pages in my calendar, has four boxes and three circles. On a good day, they all get colored in. Some days, I look up and expect to see either my third-grade teacher or my psychiatrist coming through the door to give me a gold star.

Sometimes someone will say to me, with a certain amount of wonder, reverence perhaps, considering the awe they feel in the presence of the literary production machine that I am, "Where do you get the discipline to be creative on paper every day?" Usually I make up something lofty and golden to tell him. The truth is that I write every day because I want to be able to color in box number four.

I am embarrassing myself in front of you with all of this

detail about my childish way of making myself act like a grown-up. I have been looking for weeks for some breathtaking and poetic way to say it, so you would be astounded at my discipline and insight into the ways of prayer. But here it is, such as it is— put some boxes on your calendar, and get a colored pencil.

Decide how many offices you will say each day, and check to see if you say them. To enter the kingdom of God, said the One who came, you must become a little child. I take great comfort in those words whenever I think about being the age I seem to have become and whether or not I have colored in my boxes. Perhaps with some little boxes and a colored pencil and a sheepish grin, one can enter the house of prayer as well.

Coloring in the boxes helps me get through the daily while I am waiting on the divine.

I have a friend who believes that when we get to heaven, some of us are going to have to go out behind the woodshed for a while before we are going to be allowed in. She also suspects that some of us are going to have to be out there longer than others. I do not like the way she looks at me when she tells me this.

I have another friend who spends a lot of time around people of all kinds of denominations, including denominations that say some folks—Episcopalians, like me, for example—do not have a chance in the bad place of being welcomed into the good place. My friend says that he believes there is a pouting room in heaven. It is the place one has to go if one is disappointed that some of the folks you thought were not going to get in actually get in.

There are a couple of things you should know about my friends. They both were raised in the Nazarene church, just like I was. And now they are both Episcopalians as well. Though they did skip over the Methodist part, unlike myself. They are pilgrims and not theologians. And so am I.

None of us actually knows what happens when we get to heaven, including, and maybe especially, those who are convinced that they absolutely know what the Unnamable One has in store for us, the One who has told us that we will never, while we are here on earth, understand all that is to come.

I was thinking about my friends the other day, and it occurred to me that there also may be a laughing room in heaven. Maybe there is a room where you go and discover that some of the stuff you were worried about the most actually did not matter at all. It may also be true that some of us have to visit those three rooms and some others as well. Who knows what sorts of places have been prepared for us?

Here is a general rule for people who are embarrassed that they did not say the office on Thursday the way they said they would. Even if it is the following Tuesday before they notice.

Look at yourself in the mirror, and grin at yourself the way you would at a child who had a bad day yesterday. Grin at yourself until you grin back. Giggle if necessary. Not because the prayer is unimportant but because not having said them one day is not the end of the world. It is certainly not the end of God's work in the world or in your own life. It is not even the end of your own private piety.

"Always we begin again," wrote Saint Benedict.

Yesterday is pretty much gone, you may have noticed. Today is the day you begin again. You get a whole row of fresh boxes.

For those who are drawn to this way of prayer, there is a moment when the whole business, no matter how deeply we are drawn to it, seems to be a daunting task. The time, the complication of it, the discipline required to be faithful to it, the suspicion that most days there will be no immediate return from it—a whole host of fears and doubts and uncertainties can hold us back.

It has always been this way; it is not simply because we live in the modern age.

It helps to remember that we are to be about the daily; the Divine will take care of the divine.

8

PRAYING ALONE TOGETHER

*This is my prayer: that your love may grow richer
and richer in knowledge and insight of every kind and may
teach you by experience what things are most worthwhile.*
—SAINT PAUL

The prayer of the office is in the community of saints.
—THE RULE OF TAIZÉ

*The important thing is not to think much but to
love much, and so to do that which stirs you to love.*
—TERESA OF AVILA

NOT TOO LONG AGO, THE CHURCH WE ATTEND AN-nounced its first annual men's retreat. I thought the name was pretty hopeful, actually. Since there had not been one here before, the sheer audacity of naming it as part of a series was pretty impressive. It did take place in an anno, and it was to be the only one held in this particular anno, so technically it was annual, I suppose. Of course, Sweet'N Low is technically a sweetener, but that doesn't mean you can call it sugar.

Other than that little bit of wordplay that came to mind when I saw the announcement in the parish literature, I did not pay much attention. Some of the folks who were organizing the event were surprised that I was not interested in going. After all, I am of the correct gender for the event, I am a mem-ber of the correct parish, and Lord knows I like retreats. This retreat even came with a golf outing, which rarely happens on the retreats I attend. Golf is not generally one of the habits of a monastery—but I am wondering if perhaps I have been miss-ing something there. Saying prayers before and after a round of golf might even help my handicap; it certainly will not hurt it.

The truth is that I am not much of a joiner. Those of you who are familiar with Meyers-Briggs, one of the best tools for measuring personality types and preferences, know that a twenty on the introvert scale is pretty far out there. Mine is twenty to the third power. The shadow side, the extrovert in me, that opposite part of my personality that is to be nurtured so it can bring me back into some sort of balance in the middle of the scale, recently announced his retirement. He moved to Tampa, to a place called the Home for Neglected Extroverts. He wants me to come visit, but I know that if I go down there, he will want to make conversation, and I will not get a moment's peace.

And if I were going to join something, it most certainly would not be something that excluded women. I have some political issues and some justice issues and some equality issues that come up inside me anytime women are left out, to be sure. But the real reason I am not interested in all-male events is because women are vastly more interesting and considerably wittier and generally more fun to be around anyway. "Let's get all the guys together," someone will say—and whatever they suggest strikes me as being duller than dishwater. "You boys just go ahead without me; maybe I will catch up. Y'all go hunting or play poker or go skiing or whatever. I'll just sit here on the porch and protect my wife and the rest of the womenfolk." Any of you who need a designated listener for girls' night out, I am your guy.

So I ignored the publicity about the men's retreat and even the personal invitations. Then the organizers tricked me. They asked me to speak at the retreat. Like many who spend most of their days in a small room with only a fountain pen and blank pages for company, thinking that I am thinking all of this marvelous stuff that the world ought to be hearing, I will go anywhere to listen to myself talk.

So I said yes.

I have to say that my expectations were not very high. Most of the men who had signed up were people I did not know at all. And the schedule did not have near enough silence on it to qualify for retreat, or at least as I understand retreat. (*And I,* said the guru to himself, *understand retreat better than most folks, don't I?*)

The first evening actually went okay. The folks there were kind to me while I said the things I was going to say, and the supper was good, and though there was a fair amount of the back slapping and arm punching that guys do when they get together, I managed to escape any serious injury.

The next day went okay too, though I didn't shoot a very good score on the golf course, even though I was in the group with the dean of the cathedral, which I thought would help my score some. Then one of the guys at the retreat, the only one I thought of then as a close friend, had to leave early, bringing the number of people with whom I had ever had a conversation before I got there down to four. And two of them are about as talkative as I am.

We had been saying our morning and evening prayers throughout the weekend, and so early Sunday morning, we gathered for prayers. I was a little more relaxed by then. All these good men with good hearts and kind words had finally sort of worn me down, and I was actually enjoying their company. And I had finished my work the night before, so I had exhaled finally. I was so close to just being one of the guys it was unnerving.

We gathered before breakfast in the big room with a view down over the edge of a mountain and back through and across a long valley. And the sun was coming up, and the sky was clear and the air was fresh.

Morning prayer began:

Lord, open our lips.
And our mouth shall proclaim your praise.
Glory be to the Father and to the Son and to the Holy Spirit,
    as it was in the beginning . . .
The earth is the Lord's for he has made it: Come let us
    adore him.
Come let us sing to the Lord.

And so we did.

Come thou fount of every blessing,
tune my heart to sing thy grace.
Streams of mercy, never ceasing,
call for songs of loudest praise.

In what was not one of my most reverent moments of the weekend, I thought, *You cannot possibly get these men to sing the high notes in this song this early in the morning.* I was so sure I was right that when everyone stood to sing, I just stayed in my seat on the back row, with my eyes closed, waiting for the musical train wreck that was sure to come.

I have this traveling guru, retreat leader, shy person, poet kind of way to sit in a chair that makes people think I am lost in contemplation, when I am really just trying to figure out what I am going to say next. The pose comes in handy whenever you want to observe what is going on around you without having to do something you are unsure about, like singing a hymn in public.

I got ready for the train wreck. I know what the next few bars are supposed to sound like. A fair number of us cannot reach those notes at noon, much less before breakfast.

Teach me some melodious sonnet
sung by flaming tongues above.
Praise the mount. O fix me on it,
mount of thy unchanging love.

By then, I had to look. You should have seen them, those guys. Some of them up on their tiptoes trying to hit those notes. And most all of them with their arms around the next guy. The rich ones and the rest of us, the scared and the confident, the devout and those of us who are sometimes less-than-devout, the young and the not-so-young-anymore—all standing there, holding to one another, trying their best to hit those notes in that old song of praise sung to One who is worthy of our praise at the beginning and the end of each day.

"Almighty God, you have given us grace at this time to make our common supplication to you," goes the prayer at the end of morning prayer, "and you have promised that whenever two or three are gathered together in his name, you will be in their midst."

Who would not want to be part of such a crowd? A crowd who rises in the morning and stands up on their toes to praise the One who made them, the One who made us all. Who can resist the urge to stand with them, day after day, even if we cannot be in the same room?

It was not the golf. It was not the meals. It certainly was not whatever it was that I had to say when it was my turn to talk. None of those things had us standing on tiptoes with tears in our eyes and a song in our hearts. All of those things were fine, but they were secondary to the thing that bound us together.

It was the prayer and the praise offered up that bound us to one another.

These days, given the way that I live my life or the way that it is living me, I am lucky to say the office with a crowd of folks twenty times in six or eight months. Even then, it is mostly because I lead retreats.

If you ask me to come and lead a retreat, we are going to say the office, whether you are a Lutheran or a Baptist or a Methodist, whether you are a teenager or a grown-up, whether you have ever said the office before or not. To me, saying the office in a crowd of folks is the best thing about leading a retreat. I know what the speaker is going to say already, since I am the speaker.

And even though I get to say the office with others very seldom, I am luckier than a lot of people. Most of us say it alone most of the time. And it can be hard to do.

When you begin to pray the office by yourself, there are all of these really odd little questions that go through your head. What if someone hears me? What if someone sees me on my knees, lighting a candle or sitting still in the silence between the psalms and the lessons? How odd is this going to look anyway?

What if I do not do it correctly? Even those of us who think we have unlocked the secret code of the lectionary and the propers and the calendar mess up from time to time, and we realize that we have said or read the wrong thing again this week.

What if no one ever knows? What if I am so little changed that no one can tell I am actually trying to live a life that becomes a prayer that is prayed without ceasing? What if I become a saint and no one notices?

What if these prayers do not actually matter? What if they make no difference at all? What if nothing changes, including me?

What if I am just by myself here, saying these ancient words? What if I am actually all alone?

When I left the Academy, three of us decided that we had grown so accustomed to being together and sharing such retreats that we would just have to keep going even though we had graduated.

So we met together for two or three days about three times a year for some six or seven years. Among other things, of course, we would say it together when we were together. And we promised to say the office together when we were apart as well, to say it with and for and through one another even when we were hundreds of miles apart. We promised to say the office on behalf of one another each day just in case one of us was not able to pray that day.

I have a very clear recollection of a spring morning on the floor of the studio where I used to say my prayers. It was one of those times in my life when not much was going right. And here I was, being so holy and devout, following my calling and living in and out of my vocation, doing all the stuff I was supposed to be doing, and the prayer I was offering each day was making no difference at all. I put the prayer book down and blew out the candle and said to myself, *That's it. I am done with this. Who cares anyway?*

Then that little voice, the same little voice that asks me all those questions and makes me self-conscious about saying the office—the little voice within me that George Costanza was referring to on *Seinfeld* when he once defended his poor judgment by declaring, "My little man is an idiot"—that same little voice said to me, *Well then, let's call your friends and tell them that you are not going to pray for them and with them anymore.* Just call them up and say, "I am no longer going to pray with you and for you and beside you. I am no longer going to do my part to be sure that the prayers get offered up on the days when you cannot pray."

We all love being able to say to a friend that we will pray for him or her. I suspect it is not nearly as much fun to call and tell someone that you have decided not to pray for him after all. So I picked up my book and lit the candle and rang the bell and said my prayers.

I have a friend who takes a particular chair in his living room, the same one he sits in to read the newspapers each day, and he turns the chair to face the window to say his prayers. In this odd sort of way, when the chair is facing the window, it becomes an altar.

I have another friend who says the morning office at home.

She says her midday office silently each day, while walking slowly along a circular sidewalk that goes around the great lawn in the center of a nearby university. It is the only time she walks there. She says that when she first started out, she would walk along slowly, reading the office from a book. People walk and read at the same time on college campuses all the time; that is evidently when studying takes place, so it never occurred to anyone that she was saying her prayers. Later, she said, she memorized the office and walked along saying it to herself. She had to stop moving her lips, though, because people had begun to stare at this lady who was walking around talking to herself every day at noon—which one would expect not to be unnerving to people on a college campus, actually.

I have a friend who bought a kneeler and uses it to say his prayers. He used to keep it in a closet and pull it out when it was time to pray. Then his teenage daughter took up the closet space, so now it has a permanent place in his front parlor.

Another woman I know has a particular candle that she pulls out of a drawer and puts in the middle of a shelf when it is time to say her prayers. If the candle is lit, then the chapel is open.

Every day that I fail to say my prayers, and every day that I am tempted to set the whole practice aside, I think of these people I know and their places and their habits. And I think of the promises we made to one another and the promise I made to these people to remain faithful in my prayers.

First and foremost, the Church worships the living God. It is where our understanding of God begins. And it may be the best place for our understanding of one another to begin as well.

And it cannot hurt our understanding of God or one another if we offer such worship and praise each day, rather than merely once a week.

One of my friends used to say to me, "So you want to meet God. Exactly when and where will this meeting take place?"

I cannot tell you when God is going to choose to come and be with you. I cannot even tell you when God is going to choose to come and be with me. But one of the ideas that undergird the practice of the daily office is that it is not for me anyway. It is for God. There is no more guarantee that we will have some fresh and powerful personal sense of God's presence while saying our office each day than there is that such a thing will happen to us or among us when we gather for worship on Sundays either. But that is no reason not to go to church on Sundays.

Another of the ideas that underlies the saying of the office is that regardless of whether we get anything out of the office, we are to say it in order to keep the prayer that is prayed without ceasing from actually ceasing as it passes through our time zone and city and parish and neighborhood and home.

Another of the powerful notions underneath the practice is

that it is a means by which we are drawn to attention for the presence of God.

All of those things are among the marvelous things that are part of praying the office. But it is the mundane that makes the marvelous possible.

Pick a time to say your office. There is no right time or wrong time. Pick a time.

"I need an hour. Can you not wait with me for an hour?"

While you are at it, pick a place.

The witness of the saints and the witness of stumblers like me is that where you say your prayers seems to matter. Not because the place itself actually matters, but because it is the place where you go to pray.

A candle, a chair, a certain way you stand or sit, the ringing of a bell—something done to physically say, "When I am here, in just this way, I am at prayer; this has become sacred space," seems to make a difference. It need not be obvious to anyone else should they walk into your house. Indeed, there is something about a sacred space being hidden in plain sight that I suspect would have a certain appeal to the One who said, "Go into your closet and pray." But some bit of something that will remind you that you have come apart to pray for these few minutes seems to help.

Will you always be able to be in that spot at the prescribed time to say your prayers? Of course not. We all have to leave our homes and go on the road sometimes, but having a place to call home for our prayer, an altar of some sort, will help us make the habit.

Find a friend. Look him in the eye. Promise that you will pray together even when you are apart. Write your friend's name down in your book.

It is hard to say the office by yourself. It helps when you are not actually by yourself, even when you are alone. "From now on, you are no longer alone," writes Brother Roger. And you can take others with you into your prayer as well.

The life of prayer is a solitary journey—but the witness of the saints is that you cannot, and do not, make it alone.

And then—he said with all of the fervor and wisdom that is given to those who are given the secret to the life of prayer—and then, show up.

The secret to a life of prayer, by and large, is showing up.

So you want to meet God. Exactly when and where will this meeting take place?

I am well aware of how simple and dumb these things sound. I also know that I have a place to do my work, a place to eat my meals, a place to read the newspaper, a place to watch television, and a place to sleep. And I know that I mark the passage of my days by the times that I am in those places, doing those things. And I know that the promises I have made to family, friends, and colleagues are often the only things that keep me in those places doing the things I have been given to do.

I also am aware that I do not know whether this day, or the next, will be a day when God will choose to come and be with me for a moment or two. I do know that it will not hurt for me to be in my appointed place at the appointed time. God may not have any trouble finding me no matter where I am, but it will not hurt to be where I go when I want to be at attention for the presence of God.

9

AN INVISIBLE REALITY

Is anyone among you in trouble? They should turn to prayer.
Is anyone among you in good heart? They should sing praises.
—Saint James

Let us be attentive to enter into the meaning of liturgical action;
let us seek to perceive something of the invisible reality of the kingdom.
—The Rule of Taizé

I started to sense that words not only convey something, but
are something; that words have color, depth, texture of their own,
and the power to evoke vastly more than they mean . . .
to make things happen inside the one who reads or hears them.
—Frederick Buechner

IT SHOULD NOT COME AS A GREAT SURPRISE TO YOU BY now, but I love words; I always have. I saw my name in print for the first time when I was thirteen years old and have been hopelessly hooked on words ever since.

I love them for their power to move you to tears and to laughter, to action and to rest. I love their power to transform an argument into an agreement, a hope into a prayer, a moment into something holy.

Sometimes I think that everything else begins and ends with our words. Because if you can find the right words, you can do anything.

With a few words, you can say hello or make a friend or meet a girl or say good-bye. You can stand your ground or make peace. You can hurt someone, and you can also heal a wound. You can write a song or a letter or a book or a note. With the right combination of words, you can begin to explore the world beyond yourself or find the home within yourself. You can learn the past and explore the future. You can trace the paths of the saints, and you can learn to walk the paths of prayer, and you can learn to pay attention to the Word that, in the beginning, was with God and is now with us.

And, as strange as it sounds, for a man who spends his hours and days wrestling words onto paper, I am not always willing to trust my communion with God to words of my own choosing.

I have discovered that sometimes someone else's words are better than my own. There is something to be said for listening to something other than our own sweet selves, something to be said for having to find and be found by God inside the words of prayer and worship that have been offered up by God's own for centuries.

There are some places in my life where that is especially true.

Sometimes when I travel, when I am off being the guru— which is a word that I use about myself with my tongue planted firmly in my cheek—people who come to hear me speak for the weekend or to attend a retreat I am leading will end up telling me some portion of their stories. I do not ask that they do this; they just do.

They will give me a wink and a nod, or come and knock on my door during the afternoon break, when I have cleverly built time for a nap into the schedule, or leave me a note at dinner, and the next thing I know, we are sitting in a corner somewhere or taking a walk, and they are telling me a story. They always think—because I am the guru, what else would they think?—that I am going to have some great word of wisdom to offer that will solve whatever it is that they are carrying around. And I always feel so completely inadequate and sheepish and embarrassed. I am happy to stand next to them and to listen to them, because I know it is always easier to talk to someone you are not likely to ever see again. I have done it myself a time or two.

I have learned two things over the years. One is this: the only thing I am any good at when it comes to these little walks and talks is listening. And that may well be simply because I am too shy to interrupt them and say something that I know is probably not very smart anyway. Better to keep one's mouth shut and be thought a guru than to open one's mouth and be discovered as the impostor that you really are.

But it is not me listening that matters; it is anybody listening. It is in the confessing, it is in the letting go that grace has room to put in an appearance.

The other thing I have learned is this: the things we carry around with us—unsaid, unacknowledged, unconfessed—the amount of stuff we insist on carrying around with us in that little sack on our shoulders is killing us. It is killing us literally and figuratively, spiritually and emotionally, quietly and surely.

For all of us who call ourselves Christians, there is this moment somewhere along the line when we come to grips with the fact that we are among that crowd who have all sinned and come short of the glory of God. For some of us it comes sooner rather than later, but it comes for all of us.

Immediately thereafter, another moment comes upon us, a moment in which we do our best to confess our sins, to seek the absolution which will open the door for us to begin to walk in newness of life. So then there is the moment when we stand up for the first time clean and forgiven, without sin, for our sins have been "buried in the deepest sea," as the old song says, the one they probably still sing at the church where I grew up.

It happened to me. I remember it. And there is likely such a moment that you can recall in your life as well. If you like, we can pause and reflect on how bad our haircuts were at the time, though I would rather not.

We could also go around the room and say what such a moment was called, and the place where we were when it happened to us. Being saved, being born again, having our hearts "strangely warmed," as John Wesley called it. The story of the road to Emmaus comes to mind, and the road to Damascus comes to mind too, and tamer words, like *conversion experience*. Terminology does not matter so much; it is the remembrance of that moment that matters, that moment when you knew you were forgiven.

Then we rise to go and love and serve the Lord, with our sins washed away, belonging to God now for sure in that moment. Now we can indeed go forth to live a life that becomes the gospel.

I do not have any research to back this up, but my sense is that some of us are sinners again before sundown the next day.

We put our new sin in a little sack that we carry around on our shoulders—metaphorically speaking, of course—and we haul it with us. In a few days or weeks, we have all of this stuff in our sack that we know is sin, but we do not want to admit to anyone because we just had all of our sins forgiven, and we made a big deal about it in front of a lot of folks, and God has already taken care of our sin forever, or least that is what we were told and what we even believe in an odd sort of way, the size of the sack on our shoulders notwithstanding.

So we do what anyone would do: we pretend. We pretend that all of our sins have been forgiven, even the ones we are still carrying around.

If this does not sound familiar to you, then bless you. I do not know where you grew up, but it was clearly not in the South, and it probably was not in the evangelical part of the Church. It may be that you were dropped in here among us fully formed in some way that the rest of us do not know about yet. If such a thing does not sound familiar to you, then just bear with the rest of us for a few minutes. In fact, pray for the rest of us; we sinners can always use the prayers of the sinless.

I am not interested in swapping theological left hooks with anyone, no matter where you sit on this long pew that we call the Church. There is no doubt that, as they taught me in the part of the Church I grew up in, my sins were forgiven once and for all. I do not understand that really, but I believe it is true. I also do not doubt that I belong to God forever now.

But I know what else is true. It is true that I am still a sinner, still coming short of the glory of God, and sometimes I cannot bear the weight of the stuff that I am carrying around. "Once saved, always saved" does not necessarily mean "once saved, always without sin."

John tells us that if we will confess our sins, then God will forgive us our sins and cleanse us. I have to assume that cleansing does not happen if I do not confess. If I do not confess my sins, then they will not be washed away. If I pretend that I already did that once and for all time and have no need to recognize my daily shortcomings in the category known as the glory of God—a category for which I am remarkably ill suited—then I also must pretend that I am not carrying this sack of stuff in my heart and in my mind.

If I do confess my sins, I am still responsible for changing the way I live my life. I am the one who must learn how to live in newness of life. I must make restitution when I can. I must leave my gift at the altar and go make peace with my brother when I should. I must turn around, change directions, and all of those other phrases that we hear when we talk about such. I also must not pretend.

It is easier to change direction without carrying an ever-increasing burden of the sins I do not confess. I must also learn to live with some measure of confidence that it has been done. "Absolution restores you to the joy of salvation," writes Brother Roger. "Yet you must seek it out."

If you leave it to me, I am not about to admit to anyone that I am still a sinner. Not now, now that I travel the country being the guru.

The old and ancient words of the office offer me the daily gift of the confession of my sins, a way to daily be restored to the glory of God despite my extraordinary proclivity for falling short of it. Perhaps some folks do not need to be reminded of it, but I do.

I have a friend who went through a divorce. In fact, I have several friends who went through a divorce, as I did some years ago. I also have a fair number of friends who suffer from depression as I do. I seem to be drawn to both sets somehow; there is a cosmic "it takes one to know one" notion at work here, I suspect.

If I am in a restaurant or at a park, I can always spot the guy who is out with his kids for the "dad night" he gets every other weekend. They look different from a father and his kids who are headed home to where the mother is in residence. I cannot describe this to you, but I know that it is true. If I am seated at a dinner party somewhere, I can usually spot the people who wrestle with depression; I can see it in their eyes. They can probably see it in mine as well.

Perhaps it is a publicans and sinners thing, I do not know. It is often a gift; I do know that.

My friend told me he had hated his ex-wife for a long time. He was not a particularly hateful person, and he was not particularly happy about feeling that way, but it was true, he told me.

I know this woman. I have known the two of them since they first met. It is hard for me to square the notion of writing a book on prayer and what I am going to say next, but here it is—it was hard to blame him. She is not the easiest person in the world to like.

Since this is his story and not mine, there is a fair amount of stuff that went on between them that I cannot tell you. Which is okay, really; it is not much fun to hear, and it would not be much fun to tell. It is not exactly talk-show stuff, but some of it is awful enough that you would have a hard time coming to any other conclusion.

My friend and I talked sometimes about "dad nights" and ex-wives. We talked a lot in those days about the rest of our lives too. We were both at what I think of now as the beginning of our journey in the direction of prayer, in search of some sort of ongoing communion with God.

Although the farther I travel and the more I think of where I have been, I am more and more convinced that we start on our journey toward God a lot sooner than we realize, and that we are in closer communion with God than we know, it is far more likely that we do not recognize God's presence in our lives than it is that God is not present in our lives.

But this, shall we say, lack of charity toward our ex-wives was something we had in common in those days. I am changing *hatred* to *lack of charity* here for obvious reasons. I have just included myself in the group, and I want you to think kindly of me. I trust you to do so, but I am hedging my bets a shade, if you do not mind.

In my friend's prayer each day, he had a list of those who were close to him for whom he prayed at the appropriate moment in the morning office. He would pray, as the words of his office go, "for those who had been given to him and to whom he had been given." And it was his custom not to say much about the names he said in his prayer; he would simply say the names and see their faces in his mind's eye, trusting, as the prayer says, "that you will do for them far more than we can desire or pray for." His kids were on the list, of course, and so were his brothers, and his new wife. I think I was on that list, though he never mentioned it, and I was too insecure to ask.

He told me that one day he decided to add his ex-wife's name to the list. He said that he never said anything about her; he just said her name aloud and kept going. Dwelling on her name would have been more than he could do.

After some years, he said—he did not know how many—he realized one morning that he no longer hated her. It is, evidently, hard to hate those for whom you pray. The two of them are not best friends by any stretch, he told me, but the anger and the hatred were gone.

I know the words of the office he uses. I know the words he said before and after that particular part of the prayer. I know that repeating those fifteen or so words day after day, week after week, changed him, which is, of course, one of the objects of the exercise.

Some folks might have gotten there sooner. Some folks would have pretended to. Without the ancient words of the ancient prayer, he might never have gotten there at all.

I have a friend who went to the hospital to visit a friend who was dying. The man who was dying was named Mac, and Mac was a larger-than-life sort of character. He was a record producer in our town and had been so for some thirty years. Mac had been in at the very beginning of the Christian music industry in Nashville, and there were very few people in this town in the business who had not been under his influence in some way.

Mac was about two days away from a surgery that had a very small likelihood of success. There was a better chance that he would die on the table than that he would recover from the surgery.

So everybody who had known him was going to see him in the hospital. Which was so Mac, by the way. When I went to see him, he was propped up in the bed, holding court the way he had done for years, as though this was his new office rather than the last room he would ever sleep in.

My friend went to see Mac, and of course there were a dozen people in the room. Everyone was laughing and talking and telling stories the way you did when you were with Mac. According to my friend, if the elephant that was Mac's impending demise was in the room at the time, nobody was talking about it.

At the end of the visit, Mac asked my friend to pray. Mac and his friends went to a church where, when they ask you to pray, they are often looking for a miniature sermon to be delivered without benefit of notes.

My shy friend was suddenly thrust into an extreme moment of death by sharing. One of his mentors is dying, it is likely to be the last time that he sees Mac, and these are likely the last words he will ever say when Mac is in the room. So, he told me, everyone bowed their heads, and the room got warm and uncomfortable, and my friend opened his mouth, not sure what he was going to say.

"We your servants give you humble thanks, Almighty God, for all your gifts so freely bestowed upon us and all whom you have made," was what came out.

I smiled when he told me this; I know this prayer. He said he prayed slowly, with his heart breaking as the words rose up in him.

"We bless you for our creation, preservation, and all the blessings of this life. Above all for your immeasurable love in the redemption of the world by our Lord Jesus Christ, for the means of grace and for the hope of glory. And on this day especially, we give you thanks for our friend Mac, and his life and love and witness and work.

"Grant us such an awareness of your mercies we pray that with truly thankful hearts we may give you praise not only with our lips but in our lives, by giving up ourselves for your service and by walking before you in holiness and righteousness all our days."

My friend said it got very quiet in the room, and there were tears in everyone's eyes. Nobody was even amening along with him as he prayed, surprising in that crowd. He said he decided to just take a chance and go out with the whole flourish, crossing himself and saying in the name of the Father and of the Son and of the Holy Spirit. He tacked on a double amen, partly in gratitude for having remembered the whole prayer.

I heard this story later from Mac too. He did not die the next day, of course. It was years later, in fact, before he left us. Mac was not only larger-than-life, but for a while, he was even stronger than death.

"Boy, was that a prayer! Can that boy pray," Mac said with his customary enthusiasm.

I did not have the heart to tell Mac that my friend had done nothing more than repeat the words of the General Thanksgiving from the morning office, a prayer that had been read out of a book by the faithful for hundreds of years.

Some folks would have spent their time telling God that

they did not want Mac to die. My friend figured God knew that already. He wanted to be sure, however, that God knew he was grateful that Mac had lived.

The words of the prayer had come to my friend when he could not find his own words to give voice to the groaning of his heart. That is what ancient words can do sometimes.

We had some sad news a few weeks ago. A woman we know named Brenda passed away suddenly, without any warning at all, even to her family, all of whom were with her at the time. She got the flu, and then she went to bed for a few days, and then in the middle of the night, they had to take her to the emergency room, and in a few hours she was gone.

We did not actually know Brenda very well; we had only met her once. But Brenda was the mother of my daughter's best friend, and the two girls have been friends since they met at summer camp almost a dozen years ago. When my daughter went to college in Knoxville, which is where Brenda and her family live, she even spent summers at their house while she was working and going to school. As the years went by, Brenda became a kind of spare mother to my daughter. My daughter was there for the vigil at the hospital and for all of the difficult hours and days after that.

So when the day came around, we piled ourselves into a car and went up to East Tennessee for the funeral. We only really knew our daughter and Brenda's daughter, and one or two of their camp friends whom we had met over the years. We simply wanted to be among Brenda's friends and in the room with her daughter and ours when all of those words that get said were said.

We were all gathered in a little church to say our good-byes. And there was all of the stuff you expect to see and to hear at funerals at someone else's church. There was some good singing and some not-so-good singing. There was a homily from a priest who was struggling to find words of comfort for a family who simply could find no comfort in this awful thing, and he knew it, a homily that celebrated the life of a woman he had only known for the few months since his appointment in June.

There was the chatter of folks who are too noisy in church, and the sort of crashing along in the way that always happens when people who do not attend church show up to attend a wedding or a funeral. There was the stumbling around the altar rail during Communion that takes place when a crowd of people who do not generally go to worship there are trying to figure where to walk and where to stand and when to kneel.

I notice these things—am I the only one?—and I watch for them. They make me smile, and on a day like the one we had gathered for, any little thing to smile about is a grace. Especially considering how angry most all of us in that place were for Brenda's being gone so soon and so unnecessarily, it seemed. Nothing the preacher said, try as he might, could change that.

Then I noticed something else. I noticed the words of the liturgy, and in that moment I was struck again by the powerful notion that is inherent in the faithful, careful, reverent repetition of a liturgy, words that have been said by the faithful in this very moment on this very occasion for hundreds of years.

"We commend her to you as she journeys beyond our sight," go the words from what some would call the lifeless old prayer said at the burial service. "Receive her into the arms of your mercy, into the blessed rest of everlasting peace, and into the glorious company of your saints. Grant her entrance into the land of light and joy, and a place at your table."

I could not have said it better myself, if I had five hundred years or so to try. I was grateful for the words. They reminded me of the invisible reality of the things that I say I believe in the most.

As a man who makes up sentences for a living and for a life on a good day, I am all in favor of original expression. I also know better than to count on it to reveal everything to me that I am looking for.

The "invisible reality of the kingdom of God" is clearer to me than it once was. I still see it as through a glass darkly most days, but there are days when parts of it break through on me, shining brightly in the words of the ancient prayer.

Most often it is light that breaks through in and around the things that I cannot find words for myself. Things like the sins I carry and the hatred and anger I feel. Things like my fear and uncertainty about the ways death comes among us.

The office is just a collection of words. But words are powerful things. Who knows what a single one of them might do to us over time?

In the beginning was the Word—and here is everything else now, including me and you and all that there is, seen and unseen, all of it alive with the life of that single word. From which has flowed grace upon grace.

Words are powerful things.

The daily office offers me rich, powerful, profound words that can change me and shape me. Words that have been given as a gift through the ages to me and to you. Words that can grow in me and give voice to the groaning of my heart when I cannot. Words that can teach me to be attentive to and to perceive the meaning of the work of God. Words that will lead me into a deeper and deeper communion with God.

But not if I do not say them.

10

THE GREAT RIVER OF PRAYER

I will not hesitate to remind you of these things
again and again, although you already know them.
I think it right to keep refreshing your memory.
—Saint Peter

In all things you must take your brothers into account.
—The Rule of Taizé

Things are so serious now—and values so completely
cock-eyed—that it seems to me to be of the highest moment
to get even one individual to make one more act of his free
will, directing it to God in love and faith. . . . Everything—
the whole history of our world—is hanging on such acts.
—Thomas Merton

FOR A PARTICULAR PORTION OF MY LIFE, THE ONLY REALLY good news about Christmas was that it only comes once a year. I spent some years saying two humbugs in the hallway for every hosanna in the highest. Once I married and started a family, the full weight of Christmas in America in the late twentieth century landed on me like a fully loaded minivan on the way home from the mall on the day after Thanksgiving.

Of particular concern, at least for me, was the weight of all the gift giving. To this day, my stomach gets in knots in November over the gift-buying exercise to come. I am always convinced that I am not going to choose the right gifts for the people on my list. Even though they tell me every year that I have given them some wonderful things, I have found far too many of the gifts I bought still in a box under someone's bed in March to believe them.

I am always afraid, too, that there will not be enough money to be as generous as I actually want to be. Usually in November, my banker will confirm this for me. The letters *NSF* actually mean "Not so fast, buster."

Christmas became a little more of a burden for me when the circumstances of my life changed in such a way that I was no longer living in the same house with the children I am the father of. The key word here is *divorce*, and those of you familiar with it—those who have been around divorce, and most all of us have some experience with it, I fear, directly or indirectly— know that Christmas can be hard enough when everyone is in the same house under the same roof and all of the parental units, as my youngest likes to refer to us, are pulling in the same direction.

I spent the first of those Christmas Eves alone, sitting by a fire in a field at a friend's farm about forty miles from town. I just sat by the fire all night and wondered if the Light of the World was really coming and whether it was going to really make any difference. The cattle were actually lowing where I was, of course, but it was not very comforting. I am afraid of any animal larger than a house cat, and whenever two or three cats are gathered together, I am uneasy.

Do not feel bad for me sitting there alone in the dark by the fire on Christmas Eve, though. A fair number of you spent that same night putting tricycles together and charging the batteries on electronic gear for your teenagers and wrapping shirts and ties and slacks that no one ever wore. I may have had it better than some of you that night. It is now one of my favorite Christmas memories.

The next Christmas Eve, I was sitting in the sanctuary of a fine old church. At the time, it was the most Catholic church in the history of the United Methodist Church. They had enough great black robes and a lovely enough choir and enough liturgies that even a cradle Episcopalian could be comfortable there most Sundays. Being a cradle Nazarene, I thought I was near the Vatican.

There was this moment in that Christmas Eve service, toward the end, when most everything had been done that was to be done. The anthems had been sung, the Story had been read, and the Communion had been offered and taken. We were down to a prayer and a blessing and the lighting of the candles we had been given by the ushers as we came in. There was not much left to do but sing "Joy to the World" and go home to wrap up the last of the packages. The folks in the black robes started walking in and around and through the place in the silence while we all stood there expectantly. One of them started lighting the candle of the first person in each row so that the light could be passed from candle to candle.

Then another one or two of them began moving stuff around on the table so that they could get the purple vestments of Advent off to reveal the gold and white vestments that heralded the coming of the Light. The ministers and the other officiants turned their stoles over from purple to white. The Book of the Holy Word was lifted up from the lectern while the cloth was turned over. And on and on, until the lights and the candles and the vestments, and the smiles, too, I think, had turned that great dark sanctuary into light. Not something to just hold the light—it could not be held there; the room was too small—but into light itself. I was nowhere near the Vatican, of course, but I felt closer to the heavenly host than I had been in a while.

On another Christmas Eve night, at another vigil for the coming of the Light of the World, the dean of the cathedral I now attend was giving the homily. He did not mean to exactly, but on that particular night he explained to me what was going on at Christmas when we move all those vestments. This is sort of what he said. It actually gets better every time I tell it.

"It is our turn," he said. "Hours ago, long before we gathered in this room on this night, on the other side of the world, a crowd of folks gathered to sing the songs and tell the Story and say the prayers and offer the thanks and share the Table— all of which they did to proclaim the coming of the Light into the world.

"And that great proclamation," he said, "the one made by their fathers and mothers before them, and our fathers and mothers before us, that proclamation has been heard and picked up and passed along through the night, through the dark, from town to town, from city to city, from nation to nation, across mountains and oceans and fields and forests, and now it is our turn. It is our turn to proclaim the coming of the Light, so that the song will go on and the Story will be told."

He probably actually said it better than that. But that is what I heard, and I can still hardly bring my voice above a whisper when I say what I heard that night. Some of what I heard him say that night has to do with proclaiming the coming of the Light. And some of it has to do with what is going on every time we gather for worship and every time we take the Eucharist together.

And some of it has changed the way I see our calling to pray without ceasing.

In the early days and years of the monastic traditions, as more and more communities began to spread across the desert and into Europe, such communities were often built in proximity to one another.

One of the notions they held dear was that one community's prayer was beginning just as another's was ending. The goal was to ensure that there were no hours of the day when the prayer that sanctifies the day was not being offered. There were no minutes on God's good earth when the One who made it was not being worshiped and praised.

For thousands of years, the people of Yahweh—the children of Abraham and the followers of Moses and all those who waited for the Messiah to come—offered their praise and worship to God in offices of prayer that were much like the ones that have been passed down to us. Then came the first Christians, those astonished first ones, whose heritage was Jewish and whose practice of daily prayer and daily worship was shaped by what they had learned as the faithful people of Yahweh, who was even more worthy of devotion and worship now that the Messiah had come.

Then the Gentiles, who learned the practice of the life of the devout from the Jewish Christians, took up the mantle of saying the prayers. Then the desert fathers and mothers, the people of the Church of the Middle Ages, and the people of the Reformation all took their places in the line of the faithful followers. Together they formed a great river of prayer that has rolled across the centuries, offered by the unknown and unseen saints, a great river of prayer that sustained the Church.

For six thousand years, the faithful began their days with the cry of "Lord, open our lips." They offered the canticles of praise and said or chanted the psalms. They gathered up their prayers for each other and the community and the whole world into the collects that have been passed down to us for generations. They offered their petitions and intercessions in the language of the devout, they said their confessions, and they sang their hymns.

And now it is our turn.

It is our turn to add our daily prayer and praise and thanksgiving to the ongoing prayer and praise that have been offered by the people of Yahweh for centuries. And they will continue to be offered as long as we do our part. And they may turn out to be offered not at all if we do not make sure that when our time comes—and surely our time is now—that we do our part to make sure that when the wave of prayer crosses the oceans and the mountains and the fields and comes to us, that prayer is offered up here each day, that our hours are hours that the ancient prayer is offered up to the Ancient of Days.

"The truth dazzles gradually," wrote Emily Dickinson, "or else the world would go blind."

Sometimes I feel as though I have traveled far on this road. But the truth is that in a way I am in the same place I was when I began all those years ago. Or at least I have some of the same questions:

What might happen to us if we began to pray the prayer of the ancients, "the very prayer which Christ Himself, together with His body, addresses to the Father"?

What might happen to us, within us, around us, in spite of us, and through us if we began to make these offices with great care?

What might happen to the holy catholic Church itself if we took up our places and answered the call to be among those who will offer the prayer that is to be prayed without ceasing?

I am more aware than ever of the connection between the prayer that was said in common by the ones who went before us and the daily prayer that has been given to us in our own books of common prayer. I am more aware than ever that we are among the first generation of the faithful to fail to take up our place in the long line of the faithful and say the prayer that Christ prays to the Father through his body here on earth.

I am aware, too, that first and foremost we are called to worship the living God, to pray without ceasing, to say the prayer that Christ can now only say through us.

We have covered some considerable ground in these pages.

We have remembered the simple and astonishing power of the words of the liturgy to shape us and recalled the need for us to pray corporately as well as to pray personally. We talked about practicality and discipline and obstacles. We had a glimpse of the great river of prayer that has flowed unseen for years, the river that has sustained all of the faithful of time past and will sustain all the faithful to come, including us, the ones who have been given an invitation to join in the great river ourselves now.

We have wondered aloud if this way of prayer does not somehow hold a key to the renewal if not the downright survival of the Church that we so love and that has loved us so well in return.

We have wondered what might be in this prayer for us if we said this prayer, even as we acknowledged that our worship is not actually for us; it is for the One who made us. Even so, we wondered, what might happen in our hearts and in our minds and in our work and in our relationships and in the world itself, if we said the prayer that has been given to us?

What might happen—as Thomas Merton might say to us—if we forgot our own sweet selves on purpose, cast our awful solemnity to the wind, and joined in the general Dance?

What might happen if we began to pray the very prayer which Christ himself prays, the prayer that sanctifies each day unto itself and unto the One who made us?

What might happen if we more often stood together— whether we stand together in the same room or we stand in different rooms together does not matter at all, actually—what might happen among us if we daily stood up when it was our turn to keep the song of joy and praise winging its way around the world, so that the prayer that is to be prayed without ceasing did not ever actually cease?

What would happen to us and maybe even to our parishes and our towns and the whole wide world, if we—we the Church militant, we the body of Christ, we the community and the household of faith, we the followers of Yahweh in our generation, we here at this outpost of the Promised Land—what would happen if we prayed the prayer that we have been given?

At the cathedral a few weeks ago, we celebrated the baptism of our Lord by baptizing babies. It was a good day.

On the one hand, we had the story of John the Baptizer, the voice crying in the wilderness; and on the other hand, we had the presence of the newest members of this august body, the voices crying at the baptismal font.

Welcome to the Church, little friends, I thought. *We interrupt your morning nap so that a stranger with a voice that is too loud can put some cold water on your head.*

I got the impression, just listening to the general reaction of the children who were baptized, that they did not completely understand the whole business or why it seemed like such a fine thing to their beaming parents and the beaming crowd watching the whole thing take place.

Welcome to the Church, little friends. We do not understand all of these things all of the time either.

The life of faith is not about things we understand; it is about things we believe. It is less about the things we can know about God and more about the things that draw us to God.

"Everything we learn about God leads to deeper mystery," says the old nun in Mark Salzman's novel about a convent. She is right.

We do not have to know or understand everything there is to know and understand about this ancient way of prayer. But if we are being drawn to it, we have to begin to pray it. We have to say yes to it.

We have to become attendant upon the Divine. We must do our part to see that the world is in constant prayer.

AUTHOR'S NOTE

ONE IS NEVER REALLY ALONE WHEN PRAYING THE OFFICE, even if no one else is in the room. Others are praying with you, for you, on your behalf, alongside you. I am always grateful for having been made one with the saints in heaven and in earth, as the prayer book calls them, and surrounded by their witness to the mercy of the One who made us.

The same sort of thing is true when one is writing a book. Or at least it is true for me. I am always grateful for those who are pulling for me and with me and alongside me, without whom the work I am trying to write would be poorer if it ever came to be at all.

In this case, I am especially grateful to Mr. Moberg and Mr. Daniel and Ms. Tickle, who thought of me when they thought of this series and thus accorded me considerably more honor than I deserve.

I am grateful as well to Mr. Baugher and Mr. Chittom and

all of the Thomas Nelson staff, whose hard work on behalf of my work is much appreciated.

I am particularly grateful to Ms. Stair (and her friend Ms. Terry) for their good work on the sentences and pages themselves.

As always, I am grateful to Ms. Jones of Merigold for a place to be and to write at all.

I owe thanks to the people of Christ Church Cathedral in Nashville, St. Paul's Church in Murfreesboro, and St. Francis Church in Cary for listening to bits and pieces of this work as it struggled its way into being and for being kind and gracious to the one who was trying to write it.

And I owe my thanks to all those who have prayed this prayer, who do pray this prayer, and who will pray this prayer—whoever and wherever they are.

APPENDIX A
SAMPLE OFFICE: MORNING PRAYER

MORNING PRAYER

THE VERSICLE FOR MORNING PRAYER

God said, "Let there be light"; and there was light.

And God saw that the light was good.

This very day the Lord has acted.

May God's name be praised.

THE VENITE

Come, let us raise a joyful song,

a shout of triumph to the rock of our salvation.

Let us come into Your presence with thanksgiving,

singing songs of triumph.

For You are a great God, a great king over all gods.

The depths of the earth and the mountains belong to You.

The sea is Yours, for You made it;

and the dry land Your hands fashioned.

Let us bow down in worship, let us kneel before the

    One Who made us.

For You are our God, and we are the flock that You shepherd.

We will know Your power and presence this day,

if we will but listen for Your voice.

THE COLLECTS FOR THE MORNING

Deliver us, Almighty God, from the service of self alone:

That we may do the work You have given us to do,

in truth and beauty, and for the common good;

for the sake of the One Who comes among us as one

    who serves,

the One Who lives and reigns with You and the Holy Spirit,

one God, now and for ever. Amen.

THE CANTICLE FOR THE MORNING

Blessed be the One Who made us.

You have turned to Your people and saved us and set us free.

You have raised up for us a strong deliverer, and so

    You promised.

Age after age, You proclaimed by the lips of Your holy prophets,

that You would deliver us and deal mercifully with us,

calling to mind Your solemn covenant.

This was the promise that You made: To rescue us and

    set us free from fear,

so that we might worship You with a holy worship,

in Your holy presence our whole life long.

In Your tender compassion, the morning sun has risen
upon us,

to shine on us, we who live in darkness,

and to guide our feet into the paths of peace. Amen.

THE PSALTER

[Select a psalm.]

THE SCRIPTURE

[Select a passage.]

THE PRAYERS OF THE PEOPLE

We Your servants give You humble thanks,
Almighty God,

for all Your gifts so freely bestowed upon us,

and all whom You have made:

We bless You for our creation, preservation,

and all the blessings of life;

above all, for the redemption of the world by our
Lord Jesus Christ,

for the hope of glory and for the means of grace.

We thank You, O Lord.

Grant us such an awareness of Your mercies, we pray,

that with truly thankful hearts, we may give You praise,

not only with our lips, but in our lives,

by giving up ourselves for Your service,

and by walking before You in holiness and righteousness
    all our days.

Hear us, O Lord.

THE INTERCESSIONS

We offer prayers for all those with whom we share
    the Journey:

those who have been given to us, and to whom we have
    been given,

those to whom we promised our faithfulness and prayers,
    especially . . .

Lord, have mercy; Christ, have mercy.

We entrust all who are dear to us

to Your never-failing love and care,

for this life and for the life to come;

knowing that You will do for them

far more than we can desire or pray for. Amen.

THE OUR FATHER

With all Your people on earth,

and as our Savior Christ has taught us,

we are bold to say:

Our Father . . .

THE BLESSING

Let us bless the Lord.

Thanks be to God.

Thanks be to God—Creator, Redeemer, and Giver of Life.

We go in peace to love and serve the Lord,

and to live our lives so that those to whom love is a stranger

will find in us generous friends. Amen.

APPENDIX B
ADDITIONAL RESOURCES

THE JOURNEY IN THE DIRECTION OF THIS ANCIENT WAY OF prayer is best made while surrounded by a great crowd of books as well as by a great cloud of witnesses.

The list includes resources for the office itself, for prayer in general, and for worship.

PRAYER BOOKS AND BREVIARIES

There are dozens of books that one can use; the prayer books and breviaries listed below are simply the ones I have used before and am the most familiar with. They also happen to be the ones I recommend most often.

I hasten to remind people that my liturgical education, such as it is, has come by way of the Methodist and Episcopal communions, and so my knowledge of the prayer books and other liturgical resources available in other communions—Lutherans, Presbyterians, United Churches of Christ, and so forth—is very limited. If you are a member of those communities or if you know friends or ministers within them, I heartily suggest that you be in touch with them to see if they can suggest resources to you as well.

The things I have listed below can generally be found in Catholic or Episcopal bookstores. Some of the more well-known ones can be found in major bookstore chains. Most, if not all, of them can be ordered for you by your local bookseller. Some can be found online, and I have listed the best Web sites to use.

Benson, Robert. *Daily Prayer*. Raleigh, NC: Carolina Broadcasting & Publishing, 2006. www.dailyprayerlife.com

Benson, Robert. *Venite*. New York: Tarcher Publishing, 2000. www.amazon.com

Book of Common Prayer, The. New York: Church Publishing Corporation, 1979. www.churchpublishing.org

Carey, George. *Celebrating Common Prayer (Society of St. Francis)*. New York: Continuum, 1999. www.continuumbooks.com

Community of Jesus, The. *The Little Book of Hours*. Brewster, MA: Paraclete Press, 2003. www.paracletepress.com

Episcopal Church, The. *The Daily Office Book*. New York: Church Hymnal Corporation, 1986. www.churchpublishing.org

Eslinger, Elise S., ed. *Upper Room Worshipbook*. Nashville, TN: Upper Room Books, 2006. www.amazon.com

Job, Reuben and Norman Shawchuck. *A Guide to Prayer*. Nashville, TN: Upper Room Books, 1983. www.amazon.com

Saint Bendict's Prayer Book for Beginners. Ampleforth Abbey, York, UK: Ampleforth Abbey Press, 1994. www.amazon.com

Tickle, Phyllis. *The Divine Hours*. New York: Doubleday, 2001. www.amazon.com

Hour by Hour. Cincinnati, OH: Forward Movement Publications, 2002. www.forwardmovement.org

RECOMMENDED READING

I have read a lot of books about prayer and about the daily office itself over the years. These are the ones that I turn to again and again for information and encouragement, and ones I give away again and again to people who are exploring this way of prayer.

Fry, Timothy, ed. *The Rule of Saint Benedict*. New York: Random House, 1982. www.randomhouse.com

Guilbert, Charles Mortimer. *Words of Our Worship*. New York: Church Publishing, 1988. www.churchpublishing.org

Klein, Patricia S. *Worship Without Words.* Brewster, MA:
Paraclete Press, 2007. www.paracletepress.com

Lee, Jeffrey. *Opening the Prayer Book.* Boston: Cowley
Publications, 1999. www.cowley.org

OTHER RESOURCES

• The Academy for Spiritual Formation, contact Jerry Haas,
The Upper Room, 1908 Grand Avenue, Nashville, TN
37202, www.upperroom.org/academy

• Episcopal Booksellers Association, www.episcopalbook-
sellers.org

• Revised Common Lectionary, http://divinity.library.vander-
bilt.edu/lectionary/

GLOSSARY

THESE ARE SOME SIMPLE DEFINITIONS I HAVE USED OVER the years for some of the words that were so new to me when I began the journey in the direction of this way of prayer. They are taken largely from two sources, and then I paraphrased them over the years. The people who wrote the books know far more than I do, and I highly recommend their work. One is *Worship Without Words* by Patricia Klein (Paraclete Press, 2007), and the other is *Words of Our Worship* by Charles Mortimer Guilbert (Church Publishing, 1998). Both are available in the ways that you normally buy books.

blessing–In the context of the daily office, it is another word for the benediction said at the end of the office.

breviary–A book that contains the psalms, canticles, lessons, and prayers needed to recite the hours of the daily office.

canticle–A hymn of praise or sacred song taken from Scripture.

collect–A brief prayer, most often a single sentence, that is made up of an address to God, followed by a petition, thanksgiving or intercession, and concluded with a formulaic closing.

community of saints–All the faithful of the Church in communion with one another and with Christ.

confession–The acknowledgment of one's sins before God, made either publicly or privately.

creeds–Statements of the Church's basic beliefs. The two most often used in public worship are the Apostles' Creed, the ancient baptismal creed; and the Nicene Creed, the creed of the universal Church used at the liturgy of the Eucharist.

daily office–A commonly used name for the liturgy of the hours, the ancient way of prayer and praise of the Church. It is also known by various other names: *daily prayer, divine office, canonical hours,* and so forth.

Great Silence–A name given to the hours of the night, roughly between midnight and dawn, when the last words of night prayer have been said and before the prayer that is offered at the rising of the sun.

lectionary–A cycle of Scripture readings for the Church. The most well-known and widely used such cycle is *The Revised Common Lectionary*.

liturgy–Literally means "the work of the people"; it refers to the written services, rites, and rituals for Christian worship. The liturgy for the Eucharist (Communion) and the liturgy of the hours (daily office) are the two principal worship services of the Church.

Our Father–The Lord's Prayer

prayers of the people–General intercessory prayer for the Church, the nation, the world, the local community, those in need and those who have departed. In this book, it refers specifically to the prayers of intercession and petition that follow the lessons in saying the office.

Psalter–The portion of a prayer book or breviary that incorporates 150 Psalms.

ABOUT THE AUTHOR

ROBERT BENSON is an acclaimed author and retreat leader who writes and speaks on the art and the practicality of living a more contemplative and prayerful life in the modern world. He has published more than a dozen books about the search for the sacred in the midst of our everyday lives. They range from books on prayer and spirituality to travel and gardening to baseball and the Rule of St. Benedict and have been critically acclaimed in publications from the *New York Times* to *USA Today* to *Spirituality & Health to the American Benedictine Review*. He is an alumnus of the Academy for Spiritual Formation, a member of the Friends of Silence and of the Poor, and was recently named a Living Spiritual Teacher by Spirituality&Practice.com. He lives and writes and says his prayers and pays attention for the Holy in Nashville, Tennessee.

To be in touch, write to 1001 Halcyon Avenue, Nashville, TN 37204 or visit www.robertbensonwriter.com.

THE ANCIENT PRACTICES SERIES

PHYLLIS TICKLE, GENERAL EDITOR

Finding Our Way Again by Brian McLaren

In Constant Prayer by Robert Benson

Sabbath by Dan B. Allender (2009)

Fasting by Scot McKnight (2009)

The Sacred Meal by Nora Gallagher (2009)

The Pilgrimage by Diana Butler Bass (2009)

The Liturgical Year by Joan Chittister (2010)

Tithing by Douglas LeBlanc (2010)

Stand at the crossroads and look; ask for the ancient paths,
ask where the good way is, and walk in it,
and you will find rest for your souls.
—Jeremiah 6:16 (NIV)

THOMAS NELSON
Since 1798